9/24/15
55.00

Feminism, the Left, and Postwar Literary Culture

Feminism the Left, and Postwar Literary Culture

Kathlene McDonald

University Press of Mississippi   Jackson

www.upress.state.ms.us

The University Press of Mississippi is a member of the Association of American University Presses.

Copyright © 2012 by University Press of Mississippi
All rights reserved
Manufactured in the United States of America

First printing 2012
∞

Library of Congress Cataloging-in-Publication Data

McDonald, Kathlene.
  Feminism, the left, and postwar literary culture / Kathlene McDonald.
    p. cm.
  Includes bibliographical references and index.
  ISBN 978-1-61703-301-8 (cloth : alk. paper) — ISBN 978-1-61703-302-5 (ebook) 1. American literature—Women authors—History and criticism. 2. American literature—Minority authors—History
and criticism. 3. Feminism and literature—United States—History—20th century. 4. Feminist literary criticism—United States—History—20th century. I. Title.
  PS152.M36 2012
  810.9'9287—dc23   2011046435

British Library Cataloging-in-Publication Data available

In memory of my mother

Contents

Acknowledgments

This book is mainly about culture and its role in shaping community, and in writing it I have been blessed with a wonderful community of support, both professionally and personally. The people mentioned below are responsible for all of what is good about the book, although, of course, any errors are mine alone.

Mary Helen Washington's influence on this project cannot be overstated. She generously shared fascinating pieces of information that she had learned from her own interviews about Lorraine Hansberry, Alice Childress, Claudia Jones, Herbert Aptheker, Lloyd Brown, and other Left figures, helping bring the literature to life. And, telling me that I needed to talk with a woman involved in the Old Left, she put me in contact with Dorothy Sterling, a writer and activist who was not afraid to talk about her Communist past. On hearing I was a friend of Mary Helen's, Dorothy invited me, sight unseen, to spend a weekend with her at her house in Cape Cod. While there, she plied me with stories of her days in the Communist Party, allowed me to read her unpublished memoir, and invited an old Party friend to dinner. Listening to their stories helped me, more than anything else, to get a sense of the community that existed back then; they brought to life the reading groups, plays, marches, issues, classes, and debates of which I had read, as well as the contradictions, challenges, and infighting.

Alan Wald's thorough knowledge of the cultural wing of the US Left and his willingness to share leads and ideas was invaluable, as was Deborah Rosenfelt's and Tillie Olsen's knowledge of the 1930s radical women's tradition. Special thanks are due to Norah Chase and the members of the Columbia Women and Society seminar, who provided challenging and thoughtful questions about my work on Martha Dodd and the value of recovering lost literary texts. Josh Lukin deserves credit for his efforts to make Martha Dodd a household name. And several mentors at the University of Maryland took an interest in my project that helped me visualize its applicability beyond the field of Left literature, particularly Susan Lanser, Nicole King, Kandice Chuh, Marilee Lindemann, and Susan Leonardi. My most important scholarly debt, though, is to the late Constance Coiner. Although I knew her for less than a year, she took all my unformed ideas about the connections between culture and activism and gave them shape and a home. I hope this book honors her legacy.

Lisa Nurnberger Snyder, Nancy Marshall-Genzer, and Miriam Simon provided support and friendship during the early stages of the research and writing process; they helped me remain grounded at a time I might have otherwise lost myself in the archives. In particular, conversations with labor activist Lane Windham helped me see the relevance of my work outside of the academy and reminded me of the important role that culture can play in the struggle for social change. Thanks, also, to Susan Goldstein, who helped me get my house in order at a challenging time in my life so that I could finish the manuscript.

I have been fortunate to work with some amazing colleagues in the City University of New York (CUNY) system: Page Delano, Phil Eggers, Penny Lewis, Ruth Misheloff, and the late Jane Young at the Borough of Manhattan Community College; Manny Ness at Brooklyn College; and Carlos Aguasaco, Harriet Alonso, Marlene Clark, Elizabeth Matthews, Seamus Scanlon, Lotti Silber, and Martin Woessner at the City College Center for Worker Education. Their friendship and encouragement sustained me through the many years of research and writing that went into this project, and often their work intersected with mine in ways that made me rethink some of the implications of my project.

As limited historical information exists on women and the Left in this era, and as much of the literature I discuss is out of print, my project relies heavily on archival research from the Schomburg Center for Research in Black Culture, the Library of Congress, the Schlesinger Library on the History of Women, the Sophia Smith Collection and the Smith College Archives, the Labadie Collection at the University of Michigan, the Moorland-Spingarn Research Center at the Howard University Library, the Lillian B. Gilkes papers at the Syracuse University Library, and the Tamiment Institute Library and the Robert F. Wagner Labor Archives. I am indebted to the kind and generous assistance I received from these library staffs, particularly Kate Weigand at the Sophia Smith Collection.

My research and many archival visits were funded by several PSC-CUNY Awards from the Professional Staff Congress and the City University of New York, a Presidential Research Award from the City College of New York/CUNY, a Margaret Storrs Grierson Travel-to-Collections Fund award from the Sophia Smith Collection and the Smith College Archives, and a QCB Research and Travel Grant from the University of Maryland. A Lillian S. Robinson Scholar Award allowed me to spend a delightful week in residence at the Simone de Beauvoir Institute at Concordia University in Montreal, Quebec, Canada, and to share my work with a dedicated and diverse group of feminist scholars and activists who helped me to see my project from a transnational perspective.

The University Press of Mississippi has been terrific to work with in every way possible. In particular, I would like to thank editors Seetha Srinivasan, for discovering the project and believing in its importance, and Walter Biggins, who patiently waited for my manuscript through the birth of my two children. Both of them understood the challenges of balancing work and motherhood and allowed me adequate space and time to grow and care for my family while completing the book.

Ezgi Kaya and Ruta Stulgaite took such marvelous care of my children that it gave me the peace of mind I needed to be able to finish the book. My mother-in-law, Phyllis Garland, was also an angel in this regard.

The writers in this book envisioned more cooperative and egalitarian relationships, and I have been extremely fortunate to have found such a relationship with my husband, Michael Garland, who came into my life when I had literally two paragraphs left to write for the first draft of this book. He saw it through many years of additional research, revisions, and revisioning and offered continuous support and editing. Life with him has helped me see the reward in working toward the kind of society only dreamt of by the writers here.

Max and Anna came along in quick succession just before I completed the final manuscript, and they delightfully kept me from finishing it for several more years. They have been a wonderful distraction from the work of this project, and I hope they know that they are the best work I have ever produced.

The completion of this project is bittersweet in many ways. No one would have been happier to see this book come into the world than my mother, Sally McDonald, who passed away shortly before its completion. A lover of books and a strong advocate for me building both an independent career and a happy marriage, my mother was a supporter of this project from the earliest stages, even though she did not share the politics of the women about whom I wrote. She has taught me more about the value of family and community than anyone I know, and I dedicate this book to her memory.

Feminism, the Left, and Postwar Literary Culture

Introduction

Salt of the Earth and the Cold War Erasure of a Left Feminist Culture

In 1953, a group of blacklisted filmmakers went to New Mexico to make *Salt of the Earth*, a film based on the true story of a sixteen-month strike against Empire Zinc, set within in a Mexican American mining community. Writer Michael Wilson's screenplay emphasizes the integral role that women played in the strike, showing female community members' insistence that domestic issues be included in the strike demands and their assumption of leadership roles in the union. In large part, the strike succeeded because of the solidarity between women and men and because of the support of women from nearby communities. By putting a strong female activist at the film's center, Wilson not only showed the importance of women's role in the mineworkers' struggle but also challenged the dominant image of women in 1950s mainstream culture: the housewife at the center of the nuclear family.

The choice to focus on a strike in which women were involved was intentional on the part of the filmmakers, who had various connections to the Hollywood branch of the Communist Party. In an era characterized by films that depicted Communism as an evil and marriage as the ultimate goal for women, *Salt of the Earth* was a stunning cultural triumph that paid tribute to both labor struggles and women's activism. In an article originally published in *California Quarterly* alongside Wilson's script, director Herbert Biberman and producer Paul Jarrico explain how they searched for a labor story that put race at the forefront and "that might record something of the dynamic quality women are bringing to our social scene" (Jarrico and Biberman, "Breaking" 169). The images of women in *Salt* came out of the filmmakers' desire to reflect this "dynamic quality" and the community's acknowledgment of the important role that women had played in making the strike successful. The workers and organizers involved in the strike participated in almost every step of the creative process. According to Deborah Silverton Rosenfelt, whose thorough research and oral history project chronicles the making of the film, Wilson spent a month in New Mexico during the strike and wrote about what he witnessed. When he finished, he returned to the mining community to get feedback from the workers; he listened to their suggestions and changed scenes they thought were unrealistic. When it came time to cast the film, Jarrico and Biberman abandoned their ideas about using Hollywood professionals and cast community members in most of the roles. Although the lead female role went to a professional Mexican actress, the strike leader, many of the workers and women, and the union organizer and his wife play themselves. Additionally, the union and the Women's Auxiliary contributed to the film's production, helping out with communication, transportation, and equipment, as well as food and childcare (Rosenfelt, Commentary 126–30). The community's consistent involvement ensured that the film's vision was not solely the filmmakers'. Thus, the depiction of women's role in the strike represents both the filmmakers' and the community's recognition of the importance of the women's contributions to the strike's success.[1]

While the decision to choose a strike featuring Mexican American workers was not entirely new—Popular Front cultural workers in the 1930s had striven to capture the lives of working people of color—the emphasis on women's issues represented a departure from the Communist Party's traditional approach to working-class culture. Their film reflected women's increased political participation in the Party in the years following World War II. Just as the women of *Salt* form a women's auxiliary that does more than make coffee and take notes, Communist women were taking more active roles in the Party and forming independent women's organizations, pushing the discussion of women's issues to the forefront. In her interviews with people involved in the film's production, Rosenfelt discovered that many of them "remember attending discussions and weekend seminars on the role of women" (Rosenfelt, Commentary 102).[2] Such discussions were part of a new approach within Party circles with regards to the "Woman Question," or the relationship of gender and class in the struggle for social change.[3]

Although the term "Left" has been used to describe various groups and ideologies, in this study I use it to refer to a political position aligned with the Communist Party in the United States. From the 1930s to the early 1960s, numerous organizations worked in tandem with the Party because they saw Communists as their best allies against fascism, sexism, racism, workplace exploitation, and colonialism. Take, for example, the case of Alvah Bessie. When asked why he joined the Party, Bessie replied, "I was convinced that it was the right thing to do, and I thought—as any number of people thought—that this was the only organization that was actually fighting unemployment, racial discrimination, national chauvinism" (quoted in McGilligan and Buhle 97). Today the term "Left" seems to refer to any number of progressive organizations—environmental, civil rights, women's, labor, lesbian/gay/transgender, anti-globalization—many of which have no connection to each other. But with the Old Left, the Communist Party was central. Whether as card-carrying members or as fellow travelers, people who were part of what Ellen Schrecker refers to as the Communist "movement" shared a vision of a more egalitarian world that could be achieved through socialism.

In the 1930s, women constituted a mere ten percent of Party membership. Although some women fought for gender equality, Party leaders mostly resisted their efforts. As women swelled the Party ranks during World War II, however, gender issues became more of a priority. During World War II, over fifteen thousand Party men enlisted, leaving women to take over the vacant roles within the Party and the labor movement. By 1943, women made up half the Party. The number of black women members also increased. When peacetime reconversion sent Rosie the Riveter back to the home, women fought to hold onto their roles within the Party. Not surprisingly, women were still a minority in the Party leadership, but women were taking on leadership roles within local branches and forming their own independent organizations. As a result of their influence, the Party expanded its analysis of women's issues. Whereas, previously, the Party's official position had considered women's oppression as secondary to economic oppression, some Party leaders began to acknowledge that women were oppressed in their own right. Perhaps one of the most dramatic shifts in Party policy, though, was the willingness to consider the role of culture and ideology in women's oppression. This shift, I would argue, is to a large extent rooted in the antifascist rhetoric of World War II, when women writers on the Left called attention to women's submissive position in fascist societies and argued that the fight against fascism must also be about ending women's oppression.

In the years immediately following World War II, the issue of women's oppression received unprecedented attention within the Party and wider Left and labor circles. Officials made efforts to recruit and train women activists and supported issues such as the unionization of domestic workers, equal pay and job training for women, workplace discrimination, daycare, and national health insurance. Party members debated these issues at discussion groups, rallies, summer camps (for adults and children), and at classes at Party-led Marxist educational centers, such as the Jefferson School of Social Science and the Frederick Douglass School in New York City, as well as at similar institutions throughout the country. Local branches of the Party held classes to train women to be leaders and organizers. In many cities, the Party organized annual celebrations of International Woman's Day. A Left feminist community of sorts began to emerge as women activists started independent women's organizations such as the Congress of American Women and the Sojourners for Truth and Justice and encouraged debate on women's issues in the pages of Left journals such as *Masses and Mainstream*, the *Daily Worker*, *Political Affairs*, and *Freedom*.[4] Several women connected to this community wrote fiction and drama that incorporated the Party's new approach to the Woman Question and featured militant women activists; their work was often circulated in Left book clubs and discussion groups.

It might seem imprecise to talk about the various writers I will discuss in subsequent chapters as being part of a common community. However, I use the term more to refer a community of ideas, of a significant number of people with a shared commitment to social change and a shared belief that socialism was the best way to create a more just and equal world. Thus, when I talk about a Left feminist community, I refer to the thousands of people who circulated and debated ideas about the Woman Question, black women's triple oppression, the ideological and cultural aspects of women's oppression, and women's political involvement. And culture played an important role in maintaining this community, making connections visible, disseminating ideas, and providing a vision of an alternative way of life. This book intends to tell the largely neglected story of this community and the literature it produced, as well as to explicate the role of antifascist rhetoric in shaping Left feminist thought and culture in the postwar era.[5]

To be sure, Left feminist literature had existed in previous decades. Rosenfelt traces the development of what she terms the radical tradition in women's literature back to the nineteenth century, describing the tradition as a continuous one, existing "at the intersections of the larger tradition of women's literature and the left literary tradition of writers influenced by socialism at the turn of the century, by communism in the thirties, and by the New Left in the sixties" ("Getting" 364). However, much of the existing scholarship on women's Left literature focuses on the 1930s; key works include Paula Rabinowitz's *Labor and Desire: Women's Revolutionary Fiction in Depression America* (1991), Rabinowitz and Charlotte Nekola's *Writing Red: An Anthology of American Women Writers, 1930-1940* (1987), and Constance Coiner's *Better Red: The Writing and Resistance of Tillie Olsen and Meridel Le Sueur* (1995).[6] As these works show, the emphasis in 1930s women's Left literature tended to be on women's relationship to work and the class struggle and, less commonly, on the battle against racism. In the late 1930s and early 1940s, however, there was a shift in the Party. The emergence of a Popular Front united against fascism supplanted the Party's traditional battle against capitalism. Battles against the injustices in US society were situated within a larger fight against fascism internationally.

In this book, I argue that women writers drew on the rhetoric of antifascism to critique the cultural and ideological aspects of women's oppression. In Left journals during World War II, women writers outlined the dangers of fascist control for women and argued that the fight against fascism must also be about ending women's oppression. After World War II, women writers continued to use this antifascist framework to call attention to the ways in which the emerging domestic ideology in the United States bore a frightening resemblance to the fascist repression of women in Nazi Germany. This critique of American domestic ideology emphasized the ways in which black and working-class women were particularly affected and extended to an examination of women's roles in personal and romantic relationships. Underlying this critique was the belief that representations of women in American culture were part of the problem. To counter these dominant cultural images, women writers on the Left depicted female activists in contemporary antifascist and anticolonial struggles or turned to the past for historical role models in the labor, abolitionist, and women's suffrage movements. These depictions of women as models of agency and liberation challenged some of the conventions about femininity in the postwar era. As such depictions were rare in the literature of this era, recovering these Left feminist literary texts adds a new dimension to US women's literary history.

In mainstream culture, however, the government, ad agencies, and the culture industry promoted images of women as tied to the home. Additionally, the rampant anticommunist hysteria of the early years of the Cold War characterized progressive activity of any sort as un-American. Thus this era has not been remembered as particularly Leftist or feminist. *Salt of the Earth*'s production history typifies the many difficulties faced by Left cultural workers in the McCarthy era. Jarrico and Biberman reported opposition at every stage of the production process. Under pressure from their conservative union and the Hollywood studios, crew members kept backing out of the project, forcing Biberman and Jarrico to use many workers who had never worked on a full-length movie before. While shooting, the cast and crew endured attacks by the press, politicians, the American Legion, and local businesses. The lead actress, Rosaura Revueltas, was arrested and pressured to return to Mexico, where many of her scenes had to be shot in secrecy. And in the final days of shooting, violent mobs laid siege to the set. According to Jarrico, the townspeople informed the staff and crew that if they did not leave town by noon the next day, they would "be carried out in black boxes" (Rosenfelt, Commentary 128, 130–32).

In a chronology prepared for the company's lawyers in 1955, Jarrico detailed the vicious opposition to the film's production. Once the filming was completed, labs refused to process the footage. Much of the cutting and processing had to be done at a "secret cutting room" by non-professionals. Despite these continued attempts to thwart its production, Jarrico and Biberman managed to complete the film. Yet their troubles were far from over. When they released the film in 1954, projectionists refused to run it at press screenings; and, although it received favorable reviews from the press that did manage to see it, no national distributor would touch it. The film played at only thirteen theaters nationwide, and most major newspapers refused to run ads (P. Jarrico 185–87). So, even though the film showed a successful coalition between women and labor, its production history demonstrates the challenges for Left cultural workers in the McCarthy era. Until recently, only a few copies of the film remained in print, as is the case with many cultural works from this era. As such, the cultural record of Left feminist thought from this era is almost lost.[7]

Thus it is not surprising that many people do not know about this important chapter in the history of feminism in the United States, even though this Left feminist consciousness was both radically different from feminist thought in previous decades and prescient of issues that were brought to the forefront in the women's liberation and black feminist movements of the 1960s, '70s, and '80s. In her account of *Salt of the Earth*'s legacy, Rosenfelt describes how she began to show the film in her classes after viewing it at a fundraiser for a new women's center in 1970, thanks to the efforts of Lester Balog, a United Auto Workers organizer who drove a hundred miles round trip every semester for three years to screen his well-worn copy of the film to her classes (Commentary 154). She describes her students' surprise at the film's representation of women's issues, including their desire to know, "Where did its consciousness come from?" (94). My own students have asked this same question when I show this film, or when I have assigned works such as Alice Childress's *Like One of the Family* or even Lorraine Hansberry's *A Raisin in the Sun* (which I assign as an example of a feminist text as well as an antiracist one). And this question, really, is what my book will attempt to answer: Where did this consciousness come from? How did it develop? Like *Salt*, the cultural works I will discuss depict issues that burst to the forefront in 1960s and 1970s, with the emergence of the women's liberation movement.

In the following chapters, I examine the cultural work of women writers on the Left in the United States in the years immediately following World War II. This project is not so much a work of literary criticism as an effort to document (and in many instances recover) the literary contributions of women on the Left during the postwar era and to assess their significance in terms of the history and culture of the American Left, the history of feminism in the United States, and US women's literary history. The literary texts and journal articles I uncovered through my research anticipate issues about women's cultural and ideological oppression and the intersections of gender, race, and class that would become central tenants of feminist literary criticism and black feminist criticism in the 1970s and '80s. In the remainder of this book, I discuss the development of what I term a Left feminist consciousness in the postwar era as women became more actively involved in Left politics and in greater numbers (despite efforts to contain political resistance during the McCarthy era). I will show the ways in which the shift within the Left from anticapitalism to antifascism opened up a space for women to critique the cultural and ideological aspects of women's oppression. In contrast to what they saw as a fascist domestic ideology, many Party writers championed images of women as militant activists, fighting to challenge fascism and oppression, both in the United States and internationally. Other writers linked women's activism in the United States to women's roles in anticolonial struggles worldwide, while others celebrated women's historical roles in resistance movements in an effort to show a continuous tradition of women's activism. Still others highlighted elements of fascism in women's personal relationships, offering alternative conceptions of romance and commitment. Overall, the literature produced by these Left feminist writers represents an effort to challenge negative cultural images of women, particularly black and working-class women, in American society.

These writers strongly believed that a vision of a new society must include gender equality. However, their efforts to raise consciousness about women's oppression did not necessarily translate to dramatic changes within the Left or lead to greater equality in personal relationships. Thus, I further argue that these literary texts show the ambivalence, exuberance, tensions, conflicts, contradictions, and struggles these women faced in trying to build a more egalitarian society that involved interracial and cross-class unity and emphasized cooperative relationships between men and women. These literary texts are an important part of mapping the complicated world of women on the Left in the postwar era as they provide insight into the tension of this developing Left feminist consciousness in women who were in larger organizations but were within personal relationships that were not evolving at the same rate. The literature illuminates some of the difficulties for women in navigating the political terrain of both the McCarthy era and the Left. While these literary works reflect some of the tensions and obstacles for women on the Left, they also attempt to contribute to the creation of an alternate culture by providing alternative images of women, romantic relationships, and family structure and promoting a vision of interracial unity. The work of these Left feminist writers reflects their various and often-conflicting connections to a community with a shared vision of a socialist future.

In chapter 1, I provide a historical overview of the Left feminist culture that developed in the postwar era through an analysis of the role of several Left periodicals and cultural journals (*Daily Worker, Masses and Mainstream, Political Affairs,* and *Freedom*) in providing a forum for discussion of sexist domestic ideology, women's cultural and ideological oppression, male chauvinism, and the intersections of gender, race, and class. More specifically, I analyze how these discussions took place using the rhetoric of antifascism. In subsequent chapters, I interpret works of fiction, poetry, and drama against this background, analyzing the literary texts in the context of these journals. I have anchored each chapter with key authors and texts that explore specific themes and issues raised in these journal articles. I situate the literature in relation to the writers' labor and political activism in order to construct a cultural history of postwar Left feminism.

In chapter 2, I recover the literary works of Martha Dodd, a committed antifascist and all-but-forgotten writer who lived most of her life in exile to escape charges of Soviet espionage. Much of Dodd's work reflects a Left feminist line on the connections between domestic ideology and fascism. Her 1945 novel *Sowing the Wind* shows the damaging effects of fascism on German women and highlights the central role that women play in antifascist resistance movements. Her later works make connections between fascism and the political repression of the McCarthy era. Her 1955 novel, *The Searching Light,* suggests that women best exemplified the American spirit when they participated in movements for social change, rather than remaining confined to the home and succumbing to the dominant domestic ideology. In this novel, she portrays resistance not as un-American but as the means necessary to achieve American ideals. While she places men at the center of her novels, these white men falter and fail precisely because they do not listen to the more radical voices of the white female activists, who insist on the need for coalitions with other antiracist, antifascist, and labor groups. These novels champion images of women as militant activists, fighting to challenge fascism and oppression both in the United States and internationally. As such, these literary texts challenge the conventions of femininity rampant during the postwar era.

Chapter 3 argues that Alice Childress's 1940s and '50s writings helped to educate the Left about what Claudia Jones, the Party's foremost black woman leader, referred to as the "special problems of Negro women" (Jones, "End" 51). In *Florence, Trouble in Mind*, and *Like One of the Family: Conversations from a Domestic's Life*, Childress explained these "special problems" to men and white women within the Harlem Left and encouraged working-class black women's radical activism. Through these works, Childress explains the necessity of resistance to her readers and encourages solidarity with others seeking similar goals. In the process, her characters take men and white women to task for their own racist and sexist assumptions. Taken together, these works contribute to Childress's vision of building a more egalitarian society that involves interracial and cross-class unity and emphasizes cooperative relationships between men and women.

In chapter 4, I investigate the sources of Lorraine Hansberry's Left feminist thought. Although Hansberry is without question the best known of the writers I examine here, her roots in the Communist Party surprise many people. Several recent studies have unearthed Hansberry's involvement with a Left feminist community that included several prominent black female leaders. This chapter locates Hansberry's cultural work within that community by tracing the connections between her creative works, her nonfiction essays, and the Left feminist ideas generated within that community. By juxtaposing *A Raisin in the Sun, Les Blancs*, and *The Drinking Gourd* to her nonfiction essays, this chapter illuminates some of the tensions and contradictions in Hansberry's writings and her efforts to integrate a Left feminist perspective with her antiracist and anticolonial views.

Even though the Party made efforts to challenge sexism and male chauvinism during this era, Party women did not necessarily experience the effects of this new approach in their personal relationships. When I interviewed writer Dorothy Sterling, she remembered discussing theoretical essays on the Woman Question at Party meetings but said that the theory rarely trickled down to personal relationships. As screenwriter Jean Rouverol Butler put it, "The American Left male articulated a very good position on women's rights. But he didn't live it in his own domestic relationships. There were very few exceptions" (quoted in McGilligan and Buhle 164). *Salt of the Earth* shows this gap between theory and lived reality by poking fun at the sexism of the union men and the male organizers. In one scene, organizer Frank Barnes tells the workers, "We can't think of them just as housewives—but as allies." His wife, however (played by the wife of the real-life organizer), takes him to task for not living his politics in his relationship. She snorts in reply, "Look who's talking! The Great White Father, and World's Champion of Women's Rights. . . . [W]hen Dr. Barnes gives you his cure all for female troubles, ask him if he's tried it at home" (M. Wilson 43–44).

In chapter 5, I show how what these writers considered to be a fascist domestic ideology permeated multiple aspects of society and women's relationships and how the literature anticipates the slogan from the second-wave women's movement: the personal is political. In addition to works by Beth McHenry, Sanora Babb, Margrit Reiner, Ana Seghers, Jo Sinclair, Paule Marshall, and Renata Vigano, I revisit works by Dodd, Hansberry, and Childress discussed in earlier chapters. These literary texts explore the problems created by this gap between theory and lived reality; many show models for more cooperative relationships.

The literature produced in the late 1940s and '50s by women on the Left counteracts the domestic ideology of the postwar era and raises issues that resurfaced decades later in the women's liberation and black feminist movements. These literary texts clearly point to a gap in US women's literary history. The fictional representations of female agency inherent in many of these works are seen so rarely in the more canonical literature of the postwar era. Numerous historical studies in the past decade have shown that the image of the happy housewife at the center of the nuclear family was not the reality for the majority of American women.[8] However, when I teach some of these texts in my literature courses, students are surprised to find strong, independent female characters. These texts do not gel with what they are learning in their history classes or what they have come to believe about women's roles in this era from movies and television shows. The dominant image of women in mainstream postwar culture—personified by June Cleaver, Harriet Nelson, and Donna Reed—clearly remains a powerful one. Thus my final chapter argues for the importance of these contributions to US women's literary history. It further argues that these literary texts and journal articles by Left feminist writers are forms of consciousness-raising about women's cultural and ideological oppression and the intersections of gender, race, and class, issues that would burst into the forefront years later with the emergence of feminist literary criticism and black feminist criticism. While I do not claim that there is a direct line of influence, I do want to argue for a feminist literary history that acknowledges a continuous tradition of resistance in American women's literature, a tradition that has largely been erased by the red-baiting of the McCarthy era.

This book could be read alongside several key historical studies that explore the relationship between modern feminist movements and the Old Left. Daniel Horowitz's *Betty Friedan and the Making of* The Feminine Mystique: *The American*

Left, The Cold War, and Modern Feminism (1998) traces Friedan's roots as a Left activist and radical labor journalist in the 1940s and early '50s. Dayo F. Gore's *Radicalism at the Crossroads: African American Women Activists in the Cold War* (2011) and Kevin Gaines's "From Center to Margin: Internationalism and the Origins of Black Feminism" (2002) both make a compelling case that the black feminism of the 1960s and '70s has its roots in the culture and politics of the African American Left of the post–World War II period. Erik S. McDuffie makes a similar argument but extends his analysis to the early twentieth century in *Sojourning for Freedom: Black Women, American Communism, and the Making of Black Left Feminism* (2011). Kate Weigand's *Red Feminism: American Communism and the Making of Women's Liberation* (2001) describes the impact of Old Left ideas on the women's liberation movement that emerged in the 1960s. And Gerda Lerner's *Fireweed: A Political Autobiography* (2002) describes the debt she owes as a feminist and a women's historian to her experiences in the Communist Party in the 1940s and '50s. These works have been revolutionary not only in uncovering the history of women on the Left from this era but also in showing the extent to which second-wave women's movements were shaped by ideas that were formulated by women in the Old Left.[9] This project can be situated within this larger effort to reconstruct this history; I add to this debate by showing how these writings help redefine US women's literary history. These literary texts and journal articles anticipate issues about women's cultural and ideological oppression, consciousness-raising, and the intersections of gender, race, and class that would become central tenants of feminist literary criticism and black feminist criticism in the 1970s and '80s.

As these works show, many of the ideas discussed and debated by these postwar Left feminist writers anticipate ideas generally attributed to the women's liberation and black feminist movements. However, some critics have taken issue with this effort to claim a relationship between the Old Left and modern feminism. Betty Friedan made every effort to distance herself from Horowitz's findings. After finding out that he intended to write about her Left past, she refused to cooperate with Horowitz, to allow him interviews, or to grant him permission to publish anything from her unpublished papers. This reluctance is typical; many writers and activists from the Old Left refuse to talk about their Left pasts, while others have gone to great lengths to cover up these pasts. Thus the project of recovering Left culture from this era is made all the more difficult.

Puzzlingly, some activists who proudly claim a Left past have disavowed the existence of a Left feminist consciousness during the postwar era. In a symposium in *Science and Society* (2002–2003), Lise Vogel invited several activists and scholars with roots in the Old Left to respond to Weigand's *Red Feminism*. In this symposium, several writers argue that their experiences invalidate the historical record that Weigand establishes through her archival research. Historian Rosalyn Baxandall says she is "not convinced" that the Communist Party changed its views on women's issues as much as Weigand suggests. Longtime activist Dorothy Healey takes issue with some of Weigand's interpretations of the historical record, saying that they do not match her lived experiences in the Party. And feminist scholar Bettina Aptheker argues that the archival record that Weigand establishes draws an "inaccurate picture" that bears no resemblance to her life in the Party.

In this book, I argue that the historical record does not present an inaccurate picture so much as an incomplete one. In fact, this gap between individual women's recollections and the archival record suggests a truth that was revealed in the literature of the era: that the ideas being circulated and debated in Left journals, discussion groups, book clubs, and classes did not necessarily translate to dramatic changes in organizational structure or lead to greater equality in personal relationships. Indeed, reading the archival works in dialogue with the literary texts illuminates this gap between word and deed, between theory and practice, and provides a richer and more complicated picture of women on the Left during this era. These cultural works provide what Constance Coiner, one of the leading scholars of women's Left literature, refers to as "a wedge into history" (11), a glimpse of some of the contradictions and tensions for women on the Left in this era that has heretofore been unavailable. Literature can provide insight into the history and activism of this era in a way that the archives alone cannot.

CHAPTER 1

Domestic Ideology as Containment Ideology

Antifascism and the Woman Question in the Party Presses

Fascism is determined to make women servants of the house. Democracy must encourage women to be servants of the world.

—Susan B. Anthony II (1943)

Antifascism had been a subject of Left literature since the 1930s, but it was not until World War II that women's relationship to fascism became a subject of discussion. The Communist Party established the American Writers' Congress conference in 1935 with the goal of creating a revolutionary literature in America. While the original Writers' Congress focused on the role of the worker, the political agenda in the second and third congresses had shifted to the battle against fascism. Although male authors dominated the first congress, women began to play a more active role by the third. However, despite the increased participation of women, the focus remained on the male antifascist fighter. Likewise, in 1937, writer and Left-wing activist Lillian B. Gilkes (who was also the director of the League of American Writers' New York Writers School) attempted to put together an anthology of writings focusing on antifascist movements in the United States and other countries. She solicited contributions from several women writers, including Josephine Herbst, Grace Lumpkin, Leane Zugsmith, and Lillian Hellman, but none of the stories she planned to include addressed women's roles in antifascist movements or women's position in fascist societies.

During World War II, however, this changed. In Left journals, women began writing stories about women's roles in antifascist struggles and outlining the dangers of fascist control for women. For example, in her 1943 essay, "Out of the Kitchen—Into the War," Susan B. Anthony II, the grandniece of the famous nineteenth-century suffragist and a progressive activist in her own right, wrote, "As we know, the fascist concept of women is that her life's work is to breed and feed. . . . After breeding—after having fulfilled her biological function—she is then, according to the fascists, only useful to brood over a kitchen stove. The boundary for women, under fascism, is the home; and beyond that boundary she must not go" (217). Many women writing in the Communist Party's newspaper, the *Daily Worker*, called attention to women's oppression under fascism. As one writer noted in a 1945 editorial, the battle against Nazism had also been about ending women's oppression: "The enemy, fascism, is dedicated to the enslavement of women, making them prisoners of breeding and baking" ("Woman's" 8).

In contrast to what they considered the fascist domestic ideology of Nazi Germany, many women writers championed images of women as antifascist fighters, both in the United States and internationally. In her 1942 pamphlet *Women in the War*, Elizabeth Gurley Flynn (who later became chair of the Party's National Women's Commission) outlined the many ways that women contributed to the war effort. In the introduction to Flynn's pamphlet, Party leader William Z. Foster praised women's contributions, saying,

> As in no other war in history women of all the United nations are taking an active part in the struggle against Hitlerism. This is because they are aware of the degrading fate that would befall them, as part of their people's enslavement were the Nazi barbarians to win the war. . . . When Hitlerism is finally crushed the victory will be very largely due to the courage, endurance, skill and clear-headedness of anti-Hitler women. (qtd. in Litof 11)

After the war, Party women were quick to point out that the emerging domestic ideology in the United States bore a striking resemblance to that of Hitler's Germany. They used the idea of the "fascist triple K," based on the Nazi slogan of *Kinder, Kuche, Kirche*, or "children, kitchen, church," which mandated that women should be defined by their roles as wives and mothers. Other writers used the phrase "fascist triple K" to call attention to the ways that black women were excluded from the mainstream domestic ideology. The "KKK" phrase underscored the racist aspects of domestic ideology, with its double reference to the Ku Klux Klan in the United States. In drawing connections between racism, fascism, and sexism, Party women called attention to the elements of fascist control they saw developing in American society during the McCarthy era. In addition to what they saw as a fascist domestic ideology emerging during the early years of the Cold War, the rampant anticommunist hysteria of the time characterized progressive activity of any sort as un-American. Left feminist culture from this era, then, must be looked at against the backdrop of the larger cultural climate, which was decidedly anticommunist and antifeminist.

A policy of containment, or minimizing the threat of Communism to the security and stability of global capitalism, defined American political discourse in the postwar era. Shortly after World War II ended, Stalin began expanding Soviet power throughout Eastern Europe, annexing other countries or helping them to install communist governments. His February 1946 radio address, announcing his plan to increase arms production and calling on the Soviet people to make sacrifices in order to impede "the development of world capitalism," helped set off what became known as the Cold War between the United States and the Soviet Union (Dziewanowski 284). While President Truman did not seek direct military confrontation with the Soviet Union, he encouraged Congress to pledge economic aid and military assistance in Western Europe, Southeast Asia, and Latin America in order to prevent further expansion. For the next several decades, containment policy determined the majority of US foreign policy.

Within the United States, the policy of containment extended to keeping the homeland safe from a possible Soviet attack, a threat many Americans believed was imminent. In his research on attitudes toward Communism in the 1950s, sociologist Samuel Stouffer found that a widespread fear of attack by an evil enemy, set on world destruction, permeated American culture (Worth 7). The news media helped further this sense of fear by presenting the Soviet threat to American security as a reality. Magazines such as *Look* and *Life* were integral in fostering this sense of impending crisis. Articles such as "I Don't Want My Children to Grow Up in Soviet Russia" and "Could the Reds Seize Detroit?" presented the Soviets as ruthless and bent on global domination. Newspapers presented maps with titles such as "The Bear Grows and Grows," showing a red tide spreading toward Europe and Southeast Asia. And government propaganda films presented life in the Soviet Union as lacking freedom of choice, press, and ideas.

The nuclear arms buildup between the two countries compounded American anxieties, and the fear of nuclear annihilation dominated American life in the postwar years. The film *Atomic Café* (1982), which documents attitudes toward the bomb in the 1940s and '50s, shows Americans learning to be prepared at all times to protect themselves against an imminent nuclear attack. While their fathers built bomb shelters and their mothers stockpiled canned goods, schoolchildren learned the duck-and-cover drill from Bert the Turtle. Many cities initiated air raid drills, issued metal identification tags, and built fallout shelters. Historian William M. Tuttle Jr. describes several other important factors that compounded Americans' atomic fears: newsreels featuring people grotesquely disfigured after the bombing of Hiroshima, footage of the mushroom cloud that erupted after the atomic bomb test at Bikini Atoll, and the announcement that Russia had detonated an atomic bomb. Tuttle claims that the nuclear specter haunted both adults and children, creating a "psychic havoc" that has yet to be fully investigated (21–22, 15).

Government propaganda, magazines, films, posters, pulp novels, comic books, and other forms of media helped foster this fear and hysteria. Take, for example, the government pamphlet "A Program for Community Anti-Communist Action." Published by the US Chamber of Commerce in 1948, this pamphlet warned of the ease with which Communists could infiltrate American society and encouraged American citizens to do their duty in keeping America safe: "They are a threat to you, to your home, to your community. . . . They would destroy us if they could. If we are not alert, they may do just that. . . . Communism will only be met if Americans in every *community* make this their *personal* job. It is your responsibility and your duty. You are the Minutemen of today" (Barson 145). Even the advertising industry got into the game, playing on Americans' fears and calling on their sense of patriotic duty in order to sell products. A 1950s advertisement for ScotTissue paper towels features a photograph of a sinister, Joe-Stalin-looking man wiping his hands on what viewers can only assume is an inferior paper towel. In large red and white letters, the ad asks, "Is your washroom breeding Bolsheviks?" Underneath the photo, smaller black letters proclaim, "Employees lose respect for a company that fails to provide decent facilities for their comfort." The message here is twofold: one, that American workers are primary targets for Communist conversion and, two, that the Communist threat is so insidious that even a seemingly mundane action, such as choice of paper towels, could leave one vulnerable to a Communist takeover.

Children, too, were enlisted in the battle against communism. The 1951 series of the "Children's Crusade against Communism" bubble-gum cards featured pictures and stories of Communist leaders. Number 47 in this series, "War-maker," describes the "savage warfare" of the Chinese leader Mao Tse-tung and warns that he must be stopped. Other cards profile Russian citizens persecuted by the Soviet government, such as Olga and Ivan, a "typical Russian family," who "are told where to work, where to live and what subjects they must master at school," or a soldier who questioned the government and was sentenced to death. And several cards depict cities destroyed by the atom bomb, underscoring the need to "Fight the Red Menace" that each card orders in bold black and red letters. Likewise, the "Is This Tomorrow" comic book, published by a church group in Minnesota, depicted life under Communism in grisly detail and warned on the back cover that Communism "MUST NOT HAPPEN HERE" (Barson 110–11, 157–58).

While government propaganda, advertisers, and the culture industry encouraged people to believe in the need to protect the United States against a foreign invasion, containment policy also involved efforts to eradicate domestic communism. This anticommunist crusade labeled Party members and fellow travelers as threats to American security. Senator Joseph McCarthy helped solicit public support for this campaign when he blazed onto the scene in Wheeling, West Virginia, in 1950, claiming that the State Department was "thoroughly infested with Communists" and brandishing a list he said contained the names of 205 State Department employees who were "card-carrying members or certainly loyal to the Communist Party." Within a few days, he backtracked, saying he had the numbers wrong, and, when pressed, he never actually produced a list. But he affirmed the fear that domestic communism presented a serious threat to American security, and for the next four years his allegations of communist infiltration, and the draconian measures he took to contain it, made the headlines and made his name a household word. Thus, even though McCarthy was really only a force for a few years, the term "McCarthyism" has come to represent the anticommunist crusade of the 1940s and 1950s (Schrecker, *Many* x–xi, 241–43).[1]

But while McCarthy helped garner public support for the campaign against American communists, attacks on alleged un-American activity had been going on for several years, with serious consequences for Communist Party members and union activists. Starting in 1949, over one hundred Communist leaders were arrested under the 1940 Smith Act, which made teaching or advocating the overthrow of the US government a crime. As a result, hundreds of leaders went into hiding, while others severed their ties with the Party. Thousands of other Party members were threatened, harassed, fired from their jobs, or had their social security or military benefits cut off. Those who were born overseas faced deportation, and many who wished to travel overseas had their passport requests denied (Isserman, *If* 4). The labor movement suffered terrible blows as well. The 1947 Taft-Hartley Act, which required union officials to sign affidavits swearing they were not Party members, was a "poison pill" for Communist-led unions. In 1949, the Congress of Industrial Organizations (CIO) expelled all unions that would not purge themselves of their Communist leaders. Unions which did not comply, such as the United Electrical, Radio, and Machine Workers (UE) and the Mine, Mill, and Smelter Workers, suffered from raids, harassment, and internal dissension (Georgakas 767–68).[2]

The House Un-American Activities Committee (HUAC), originally formed in 1930 to fight Communism within the United States, played a significant role in the anticommunist crusade. HUAC became a permanent subcommittee in 1945. Under the leadership of chairman J. Parnell Thomas, HUAC used its authority to investigate communist influence in progressive political and cultural organizations. Thousands of people were hauled before HUAC, sometimes for actual Party involvement but more often for association with any progressive cause. Many people were summoned to testify against acquaintances, even if they themselves were not involved. Charged with accusations and forced to answer the dreaded question, "Are you now or have you ever been a member of the Communist Party?" many people collapsed under the pressure and named names, while those who refused went to jail or faced the loss of their careers.

Black leaders and organizations working in connection with the Party also came under attack. The performing artist and political activist Paul Robeson faced vicious repression. According to his biographer Martin Bauml Duberman, Robeson did not belong to the Party, but he considered the Communists to be his best allies in struggles against racism, fascism, and colonialism both within the United States and internationally (337–38, 418). Because of his work with the Party, he was attacked by the government and the press, had his passport revoked, and was prevented from performing. Perhaps the most virulent example of the link between anticommunism and antiracism is the 1949 Peekskill riots, a series of violent attacks against attendees of a benefit concert for the Harlem chapter of the Civil Rights Congress, at which Robeson was the intended headliner. The Peekskill Junior Chamber of Commerce decried the concert as pro-Communist and turned out demonstrators to try to stop it. Before the concert even began, a group of armed vigilantes brutally attacked the crowd, overturning cars and vendor stands. Thirteen people were seriously injured. The police finally intervened, but the concert was canceled before Robeson arrived. Outraged at the events, the black community vowed to fight back, and leaders planned another concert. Local unions provided security for Robeson, and over 20,000 people attended. After the concert ended, protestors stoned the departing concertgoers; over 140 people were injured. Although Robeson and other leaders tried to press charges, a federal court dismissed their case. Author Howard Fast describes the riots as "the first great open manifestation of American fascism" (quoted in Boyd 572–73).

While Robeson's case is the most severe, other black activists were also threatened and persecuted. Ben Davis, a leader in the Harlem community, was convicted under the Smith Act and driven from his city council seat. The militant black leader W.E.B. Du Bois was repeatedly harassed and intimidated; he and his wife, Shirley Graham, had their passports revoked. Claudia Jones, the Party's foremost black woman leader, was jailed under the Smith Act and deported to England. Lorraine Hansberry, who took Robeson's place at an international peace conference in Uruguay when he could not travel because his passport has been revoked, had her own passport revoked when she returned. In *Scandalize My Name: Stories from the Blacklist* (2000), a documentary featuring interviews with black artists and activists from the McCarthy era, actor Ossie Davis talks about the use of anticommunist rhetoric to discredit antiracist activity. Of the blacklist, he says, "We didn't know if we were on the list because we were black or because we were Red." Davis and the other activists interviewed for the project insist that the involvement of black activists with the Party was used to discredit any antiracist work—such as integration, anti-lynching, or voting rights—as communist agitation.

The anticommunist crusade severely fragmented the Left, and the repercussions of the anticommunist crusade extended beyond the individuals and organizations involved. By creating a fear of voicing dissent, McCarthyism engendered support of consensus to a white, middle-class, and conservative status quo. Because the costs of being labeled un-American were so great, conformity became the norm, the only safe thing to do. Larry May refers to this pressure to conform as an "ideology of consensus." He claims that this ideology profoundly transformed mainstream notions of American identity and the American Dream by fostering the belief that America was, finally, becoming a classless society. The quest for a private home and a stable family life became the epitome of the American Dream, May claims, and belief in this new middle class elided the profound racial, sexual, and class inequalities in American society (5, 11–12). Thus, patriotism became equated with maintaining the imagined status quo, rather than addressing the inequalities in American society.

This pressure to conform had specific consequences for women. As Elaine Tyler May argues persuasively in *Homeward Bound: American Families in the Cold War Era* (1999), a domestic ideology developed alongside containment policy, an ideology that dictated specific and limited roles for women in the postwar era. During World War II, many women were called into service to support the war industry. Working-class and black women were given jobs traditionally reserved for men, and an image of the independent women—as epitomized by Rosie the Riveter—was championed. Although women workers still made a fraction of the salary of men in similar jobs, women enjoyed economic opportunities that had been denied to them in previous eras. After World War II, with the reconversion to a peacetime economy, women found themselves replaced by men in most of the industry jobs. But a change also took place in terms of American domestic ideology in the postwar era. The anxieties of the Cold War and the fear of nuclear annihilation and a Soviet takeover created the need for security and stability. And this need manifested itself most visibly in the need for a secure home life. May writes, "The home represented a source of meaning and security in a world run amok;" with the United States on "moral alert" against internal subversion, women's domestic roles were imbued with a sense of "national purpose" and "civic virtue" (*Homeward* 18, 82, 89). According to this ideology, the way to be a good woman—and thus a good American—was to find contentment in the role of wife, mother, and homemaker.

This view of femininity and family was frequently enlisted in the battle against communism. May describes how the image of woman as mother and homemaker was used to defend the American way of life. She writes that, along with childbearing, "domesticity was not so much a retreat from public affairs as an expression of one's citizenship" (*Homeward* 141). Soviet women, in contrast, were frequently depicted as drab, unattractive, and uncaring women who left their children in state-sponsored daycare centers while they toiled in factories. The Soviet woman worker symbolized the potential for undermining the harmony and stability of American society, whereas the United States was safe because American women had the freedom to stay at home and maintain the sanctity of the family. As cosmetics manufacturer Veronica Dengel tells readers in a *New Yorker* profile, "We are safe from Communism and all other 'isms' as long as our women can wear beauty like a badge of courage" (71).

May claims that then-vice-president Richard Nixon reinforced the connection between femininity and anticommunism when he visited the Soviet Union in 1959 for the opening of the American National Exhibition in Moscow. In what became known as the "kitchen debate," Nixon and Soviet premier Nikita Khrushchev engaged in a lengthy verbal battle over the virtues of American life as opposed to life under Communism. According to May's description of the debate, Nixon "proclaimed that the 'model' home, with a male breadwinner and a full-time female homemaker, adorned with a wide array of consumer goods, represented the essence of American freedom" (*Homeward* 10–11). This celebration of women's role at the center of the nuclear family equated women who worked outside of the home as threats to a stable society. Within this context, women who did not fit the ideal were viewed not only as unfeminine but also as threats to American security and, therefore, most decidedly un-American.

The rise of television in the postwar era also helped perpetuate this feminine ideal. Television shows such as *Leave It to Beaver, Ozzie and Harriet,* and *Father Knows Best* depicted white, middle-class families with mothers cheerily tending the home fires and overseeing the children's daily activities while the fathers provided the necessary income to support the families' suburban lifestyles. When black women appeared at all on TV, they were cast as domestic workers in white households, devoted to cleaning the homes and taking care of the children of their white employers. The few programs featuring working-class women cast them in comic roles, presenting them in conflict with their husbands. And lesbians were entirely excluded, as were single and divorced women. The three best-selling women's magazines, *Ladies Home Journal, Woman's Home Companion,* and *McCall's,* presented a similar unified image of American women's lives.[3] The pages of these glossy magazines encouraged women to conform happily to their roles as wives and mothers, giving advice on child rearing and keeping husbands happy. Photos overwhelmingly featured white, heterosexual women in suburban communities, and rarely did these magazines address the concerns of mothers who had to (or chose to) work outside of the home.

Women who did not fit the image of the white, middle-class, heterosexual, married mother and homemaker were presented as threats to a stable society. In movies, independent women were commonly depicted in the form of the femme fatale, a devastatingly gorgeous and cunning woman who could destroy men. In films like *I Married a Communist* and *The Red Menace,* communists used seductive women to lure unsuspecting men to the Party. The femme fatale image was common in fiction, too. May describes the protagonist of Philip Wylie's novel *Smoke across the Moon* as "a sexually liberated left-wing woman" who "encourages communist infiltration and destroys men" (*Homeward* 84–85). As female sexuality had the power to destroy men, May argues, it therefore had to be contained within the marriage.

Not only were lesbians excluded from the feminine mystique, but also their lack of conformity was often considered un-American. Elsewhere, Elaine Tyler May describes homophobia in the Cold War era: "ferocious, destroying careers, encouraging harassment, and forcing homosexuals to name others with whom they associated. . . . Lesbians who were open about their identity faced extreme hostility and even violence" (*Pushing* 95–96). The federal government, the State Department, and the Civil Service fired thousands of gay men and lesbians during the 1950s, equating homosexuality with Communism. In *The Culture of the Cold War* (1996), historian Stephen J. Whitfield describes the widespread belief among government employers that lesbians and gay men were security risks because "they were so readily susceptible to seduction" and "were easily drawn to subversive organizations." In 1950, the Senate released *Employment of Homosexuals and Other Sex Perverts in Government*, a report that warned, "One homosexual can pollute a Government office" (Whitfield 43–44). The fear of homophobic violence kept many lesbians in the closet or else forced them into unhappy marriages.

Betty Friedan's *The Feminine Mystique*, published in 1963, perhaps best describes the acceptable image for women in the 1950s, an image that Friedan insists is part of a propaganda campaign that encouraged women to seek fulfillment in their roles as wives and mothers, rather than in the outside world. She claims that books and magazines taught women "that truly feminine women do not want careers, higher education, political rights. . . . All they had to do was devote their lives from earliest girlhood to finding a husband and bearing children" (16). The power of the feminine mystique lay in its ability to make women believe their failure to conform to this image was due to their own shortcomings. Women of color, working-class women, lesbians, single women, female activists, and women who pursued higher education or careers were stigmatized for not fitting the image of the white, middle-class, suburban housewife. Even though economic, racial, and sexual barriers prevented most Americans from living out the American Dream of which Nixon boasted to Khrushchev, women who did not or could not conform to the feminine mystique were judged by their failure to live up to the ideal. The prevailing domestic ideology thus doubly stigmatized female activists on the Left: they risked being labeled un-American both for their political involvement and their rejection of the homemaker role.

Friedan herself managed to escape the un-American stigma by constructing herself in *The Feminine Mystique* as an unhappy homemaker, bored with her domestic suburban lifestyle. However, historian Daniel Horowitz has carefully traced Friedan's roots as a Left activist and radical labor journalist in the 1940s and early 1950s. In *Betty Friedan and the Making of* The Feminine Mystique: *The American Left, the Cold War, and Modern Feminism* (1998), he reports that from 1946 to 1952, she wrote for *UE News*, the official publication for the United Electrical, Radio and Machine Workers of America (UE), one of the most radical unions in the postwar era. Expelled from the CIO for it refusal to rid itself of Communist leaders, UE fought for the rights of black and women workers. Her 1952 pamphlet, *UE Fights for Women Workers*, argued for the need to improve women's pay and working conditions and challenged stereotypical assumptions about women's roles in American society. In 1953, she published *Women Fight for a Better Life! UE Picture Story of Women's Role in American History*, a pamphlet that championed the role of black, working-class, and activist women in struggles for peace and justice (Horowitz 121, 138–39).

Horowitz's research suggests that Friedan's *The Feminine Mystique* was rooted in the Left feminist struggles of the 1940s and '50s. And, indeed, many of the ideas in the book can be traced to the Left's critique of domestic ideology in the 1940s and '50s. While Friedan later distanced herself from her Left past, she was connected to a Left feminist community that fought to advance women's issues despite this repressive political climate, both by establishing independent women's organizations and by writing in the pages of the Party presses.

In 1945, the Communist Party reestablished its National Women's Commission, which had been disbanded in 1940. In her role as chair of this commission, Elizabeth Gurley Flynn advocated on behalf of the thousands of women who had found wartime employment. She encouraged women to fight to keep their jobs and government-sponsored day care and argued that the Party should organize around women's workplace issues (Baxandall, *Words* 50). In her 1947 pamphlet, *Women's Place—in the Fight for a Better World*, Flynn reached beyond Party circles to recruit working-class and black women to the Party. Throughout the pamphlet, she accentuated the gains that women had won through their participation in revolutionary labor and peace movements and encouraged women's militant activism around issues of peace, housing, equal pay, day care, and voting rights. She also used her influence to encourage Party leaders to take women's issues more seriously. Her efforts were bolstered by the increased numbers of women who had joined the Party ranks during the war, but the Party began to value women's participation more highly as McCarthyism began to fragment the Left. By 1948, after a number of leaders had been arrested under the Smith Act and the Taft-Hartley Act threatened to erode labor support for the Party, women's participation became crucial to the Party's survival. Party officials began expanding their efforts to recruit women organizers and develop women leaders (Weigand 71–80).

Historian Rebecca Hill argues that the Party's switch on gender issues was also due to the influence of "a significant group of black women [who] had been building their strength since 1935 through the National Negro Congress (NNC)" (72). Formed during the Great Depression, the NNC worked closely with the Party to fight against workplace discrimination, lynching, and police brutality. The Party established a reputation during the 1930s for supporting antiracist struggles and working to recruit and train black organizers. In the 1931 Scottsboro case, the Party and the NNC waged an extended legal battle on behalf of the nine black men who had been accused of raping two white women. Throughout the 1930s and '40s, the Party helped organize African American workers in the South and in northern cities, and it had a strong base of support within the Harlem community.

Claudia Jones, who later became the secretary of the National Women's Commission, became involved with the NNC and the Party due to her work on the Scottsboro defense. Along with Thelma Dale, she became a leader in the Harlem Left, and both fought to keep black women's issues at the forefront of the NNC's agenda. In the late 1930s, according to Hill, the NNC was ahead of the Party in its analysis of gender issues, largely due to Dale's efforts as NNC executive secretary. Dale publicly criticized NNC leaders for their sexism. She also spoke out in support of black women in unions, called for the unionization of domestic workers, and criticized Hollywood's representations of blacks in movies. After World War II, Jones took up the charge led by Dale and helped to put black women's issues on the Party agenda (Hill 73).

In 1946, an interracial group of women founded the Congress of American Women (CAW), the first independent women's organization endorsed by the Party. Amy Swerdlow claims that the Party's "support of an independent broad-based separatist women's movement, not a woman's auxiliary of a labor union or a woman's division of a party-controlled mass organization, was something new" (300). The CAW emerged out of a conference of the Women's International Democratic Federation (WIDF), an antifascist coalition representing tens of millions of women from forty-one countries. The thirteen American delegates to the conference were ethnically diverse; Dale was among the delegates. Galvanized by the stories of women's resistance to fascism throughout Europe, these thirteen women started the CAW when they returned. By the end of its first year, the CAW had a membership of 250,000. Although the membership was not limited to the Communist Party, many of the leaders—including Flynn and Jones—were leaders in both organizations (Swerdlow 297–99, 302).

The CAW's agenda included equality in the workplace and job training for black and white women, child care, and national health insurance. While these demands were primarily economic, the CAW was first and foremost opposed to "fascism in any form at home or abroad" (Congress of American Women, *Ten* 1). As part of the fight against fascism, the CAW also protested negative cultural representations of women. In her account of the group's achievements, Swerdlow cited a 1946 CAW report that acknowledged "the importance of such misrepresentation in influencing public opinion against women's right to a free and equal place in America" and resolved that the CAW should "act as a watchdog of these misrepresentations and take proper action to correct them" (304). Because of its emphasis on the recruitment and grassroots organizing of black and working-class women, the CAW was successful at building coalitions with diverse groups of women. Although Claudia Jones and other black leaders often criticized the CAW for its white chauvinism, Jones also praised the "tremendous participation" of black women (qtd. in Swerdlow 430). Swerdlow claims the CAW "had a larger number of black women among its officers than any other feminist or mixed-gender peace organization before the 1940s or since" (300). By 1950, McCarthyism had destroyed the CAW, but it served as a successful model of coalition politics that many of its members continued to employ in their Party work in the early 1950s.

Another important women's organization, the Sojourners for Truth and Justice, coordinated black women's political activities on a national level. The leadership was made up almost entirely of pro-Communist women, including Jones and Alice Childress. Founded in September 1951, the group lobbied the federal government to address lynching and racial violence. The Sojourners also took up the cause of Rosa Lee Ingram, a black woman sharecropper jailed for defending herself against the white man who tried to rape her (the CAW also fought on Ingram's behalf).[4] In October 1951, the Sojourners sponsored a rally in Washington, D.C. A coalition of trade unionists, domestic and factory workers, government workers, PTA members, and students from around the country came to Washington to demand that government officials address racial hatred and violence. Women all over the country donated their paychecks and rent money in order to send representatives on the sojourn. Their proclamation read, "In the spirit of Harriet Tubman and Sojouner Truth, we demand the death of Jim Crow!" While Jones was not permitted to travel due to her Smith Act conviction, a young Lorraine Hansberry—who had recently moved to New York and was living with Jones—traveled to Washington to attend the rally (Hansberry, "Women" 8).

Women's increased political participation in independent organizations and local branches pushed the Party to expand its analysis of the Woman Question. Additionally, the publication of Betty Millard's *Woman against Myth* pamphlet in 1948 sparked a debate within the Party that challenged members to rethink women's oppression under capitalism (Weigand 8). Millard described many of the economic, legal, and political barriers to women's equality and asserted that women were also hindered by the sexist ideology of a male supremacist society. "It is hardly remarkable," she wrote, "that the great majority of women are from earliest childhood convinced—if only subconsciously—of their inferiority to men." Millard concluded by arguing that the Party had a responsibility to develop "a conscious political philosophy and program designed to bring women into equality" (5–7, 22). In response, the Party formed a commission to issue a report on Millard's pamphlet and to define the position the Party would take on women's oppression. Claudia Jones published the first response to Millard's pamphlet. In "For New Approaches to Our Work among Women," Jones argued that the Party needed to make the Woman Question a "'must' for every party member" and outlined a specific program that the Party should follow, including organizing black women workers and providing childcare services so that women could become more actively involved in Party activities (741–42). Three months later, the commission published "On Improving the Party's Work among Women," its official response to Millard's pamphlet. Published under the name of Party chairperson William Z. Foster in order to give it legitimacy, the report affirmed Millard's analysis and established the Party's newfound commitment to supporting women's issues and challenging male supremacy (Weigand 86).

While Millard's pamphlet inspired change in the Party's consideration of the relationship between gender and class oppression, Claudia Jones incited Party members to analyze and address the specific problems facing black women. In 1949, *Political Affairs* published Jones's "An End to the Neglect of the Problems of the Negro Woman!" In this article, Jones argued that black women suffered "degradation and super-exploitation" because they were triply oppressed: as blacks, as women, and as workers. This term "triple oppression" was used widely in the *Daily Worker* and in *Political Affairs;* it became a catch phrase for describing the interlocking oppressions of gender, race, and class. Jones addressed the need for the Left to pay attention to the "special problems" of black women, asserting that "only the Communist Party . . . can achieve for the Negro Women—for the entire Negro people—the full equality and dignity of their stature in a Socialist society." She called on whites in the Party to initiate discussions with regards to black women's roles and to recruit black women into organizing and leadership positions ("End" 51–52, 66–67). The National Women's Commission republished the article as a pamphlet in 1949. Jones's article forced Party members to address the ways that black women were specifically affected by the fascist domestic ide- ology. Largely in response to Jones's article, the Party worked to educate mem- bers about her ideas and to expand its efforts to attract black women (Weigand 107).

In her article, Jones also tore into white women for their treatment of black women, accusing them of chauvinism, "often expressed in their failure to have close ties of friendship with Negro women and to realize that this fight for equal- ity of Negro women is in their own self-interest, inasmuch as the super-exploi- tation and oppression tends to depress all women." As examples of chauvinism, she included white women's assumption that all black women must be domestic workers: "Chauvinistic expressions also include paternalistic surprise when it is learned that Negroes are professional people. . . . Then, there is the reverse prac- tice of inquiring of Negro women professionals whether 'someone in the family' would like to take a job as a domestic worker" ("End" 60, 61–62). According to Weigand, while some white women accused Jones of "the most awful reverse chauvinism," her article pushed them to question their racial politics (107).

In this and other articles, Jones argued that the dominant domestic ideol- ogy was fascist not only because it mandated an inferior role for women but also because the "woman" represented in the mainstream culture industry was invariably white and middle class. Black and working-class women were thus relegated to a sub-inferior status. Jones argued that black women are misrepre- sented in the cultural realm, where the black woman "is the victim of the white chauvinist stereotype as to where her place should be. In the film, radio, and press, the Negro woman is not pictured in her real role as breadwinner, mother, and protector of the family." She emphasized black women's contributions to mass movements, asserting, "Negro women are the real active forces—the or- ganizers and workers—in all the institutions and organizations of the Negro people." At the end of her article, she called on Left cultural workers to "write and sing of the Negro woman in her full courage and dignity" ("End" 55, 64). Weigand rightly notes that Jones was instrumental in the Party's efforts to reclaim black women's history. Although Herbert Aptheker and a few other Communist historians had researched black women's history prior to Jones's article, Weigand claims that only after its publication did Communists take seriously the project of chronicling the activism and leadership of black women historical figures such as Sojourner Truth, Harriet Tubman, Ida Wells-Barnett, Frances Harper, Mary Church Terrell, Mary McLeod Bethune, Harriet Jacobs, Maggie Lena Walker, and Moranda Smith (109). Alice Childress's musical review *Gold Through the Trees* (1952), which depicted women's participation in several centuries of the black liberation movement, and Lorraine Hansberry's television script *The Drinking Gourd*, which depicts a fictional slave mother who challenges the institution of slavery, can be seen as part of this larger project. As subsequent chapters will show, Jones's article clearly influenced the representations of women in the work of both Childress and Hansberry.

This willingness to consider the role of culture and ideology in women's oppression represented a dramatic shift in Party policy, a shift that is largely rooted in the Party's use of antifascist rhetoric, both during World War II and in the early years of the Cold War. During World War II, many women wrote stories in the *Daily Worker* about women's roles in antifascist struggles and called attention to women's submissive position in fascist societies. As one writer noted in a 1945 editorial, the battle against Nazism had also been about ending women's oppression: "The enemy, fascism, is dedicated to the enslavement of women, making them prisoners of breeding and baking" ("Woman's" 8). After the war, women writers on the Left used similar language to describe the developing domestic ideology in the United States and argued that women's oppression was maintained and reinforced through fascist culture and ideology. Party women used the idea of the "fascist triple K," based on the Nazi slogan of *Kinder, Kuche, Kirche*, or "children, kitchen, church," which mandated that women should be defined by their roles as wives and mothers. In "Hitler's 3 K's for Women—An American Rehash" (1947), Flynn critiqued the ideas in *Modern Woman: The Lost Sex* (1947), a best-selling book by Marynia F. Farnham and Ferdinand Lundberg that urged women to return to the home for the good of their country and attributed women's desire for equality to psychological problems. Throughout the article, she juxtaposes statements from the book with statements from Hitler, but she ends by warning readers that this book is not the only culprit: "There is a veritable flood of such books and articles attacking the modern American woman. The stench of fascism arises from them. This happened in Germany when Hitler came to power. Back to the kitchen, the brothel, the menial tasks, breed the master race—are the degrading concepts of women inherent in fascism" (208). Foster's 1948 *Political Affairs* article, which outlined the Party's new approach to the Woman Question, acknowledged the need to challenge the fascism of American domestic ideology, thus legitimizing the project of addressing women's ideological and cultural oppression.

Other writers, including Jones and Dale, used the phrase "fascist triple K" to call attention to the ways that working-class and black women were excluded from the mainstream domestic ideology. In a 1949 *Worker* article, Jones discussed "the new twist given to these anti-woman prejudices, which range from male domination of woman in the home to women's 'psychological' inferiority. . . . These 'theories' are designed to divert women from progressive struggle and to reduce her to the fascist Kinder-Kuche-Kirche level" ("We" 11). The "KKK" phrase underscored the racist aspects of domestic ideology, with its double reference to the Ku Klux Klan in the United States. In drawing connections between racism, fascism, and sexism, Party women called attention to what they saw as fascist aspects of American society and culture.

Margrit Reiner's 1952 article, "The Fictional American Woman: A Look at Some Recent Novels," examines the ways best-selling novels and book club selections perpetuate the current domestic ideology. She refers to working-class and black women as "forgotten heroine[s]," declaring, "With a few notable exceptions the working-class women appear mainly as domestic workers or 'comic relief'—queer, uncouth, peculiar people. This is especially glaring in the depiction of Negro women." She goes on to argue that if such women were depicted realistically, writers and readers "would immediately have to face up to the issues of economic dependence, limited job opportunities, lower wages, absence of child care and health facilities, and educational restrictions" (1, 2). In addition to claiming that most novels perpetuate a distorted view of femininity and ignore the inequalities in American society, she decries the absence of black and working-class women in these novels. She describes Myra Page's *Daughter of the Hills* (originally published as *With Sun in Our Blood*, 1952) as a step "in the right direction" and cites Dolly Hawkins, the heroine of the novel, as an alternative to the dominant image of femininity in 1950s fiction. Reiner claims, "Certainly the Dolly Hawkinses in our country deserve the attention of many other creative talents, for in their lives they embody the power and richness of the working class." She also praises Lloyd Brown's *Iron City* (1951) as an "outstanding" portrayal of "strong and militant" black female characters (9, 10).

Helen Lazarus's "What's New in Women's Magazines" (1954) makes a similar critique of the representation of women in popular women's magazines (*Ladies' Home Journal, Women's Home Companion, McCall's, Women's Day,* and *Good Housekeeping*), claiming they target middle-class white women and exclude "the 'forgotten woman,' the working-class woman, the farm wife, the Negro and foreign born" (41). She further argues that the magazines strive to reinforce the dominant domestic ideology by "speak[ing] of woman's role as primarily a reproductive one, devoted to the service of husband and home" (45) and calls for such magazines to reflect the current reality for most women, who work out-side of the home. She also acknowledges the need for childcare facilities, both to improve working conditions for working-class women and also so that middle-class women suffering from "the boredom of idleness" (45) can work outside the home if they so choose.

The filmmaker John Howard Lawson (a section leader in the Hollywood branch of the Party and a member of the Hollywood Ten) extended the critique of the domestic ideology to the movie industry. In a section on "The Degrada-tion of Women" in his *Film in the Battle of Ideas* (published by the *Masses and Mainstream* press in 1954), he writes, "Hollywood treats 'glamor' [sic] and sex appeal as the sum-total of woman's personality. . . . It is assumed that women are less 'reasonable' than men, more 'instinctual,' less able to suppress 'primi-tive' impulses. . . . [I]ntellectually and morally, she is inferior" (61–62). Lawson later connects these negative representations of women to "Hitler propaganda in Germany," claiming, "These are men whose way of life is based on contempt for women" (63).

Other Left writers wrote stories featuring female activists as a way to counter what they considered fascist images of women in the mainstream culture indus-try. Articles in the *Daily Worker* encouraged women readers to join the Party and become politically active, printing sketches of women activists in Spain, Poland, Italy, Romania, and the Soviet Union. *Masses and Mainstream*, the Party's cul-tural journal, published fiction by and about women antifascist fighters in other countries, presenting a gendered experience of resistance movements and ex-panding the critique of domestic ideology to an international setting. Both pub-lications also published articles comparing women's position under capitalism in the United States to that of women in socialist societies. One *Worker* column describes social services for working mothers in Czechoslovakia, including free maternity care and paid maternity leave, childcare facilities, housecleaning and cooking cooperatives, and health insurance. The column concludes that these services have enabled women "to participate fully in the life of the community and the country" ("What" 11). A *Masses and Mainstream* article declares, "In its provision for the care of mothers and children a socialist society exemplifies its regard for all human life," and addresses the need for "a comprehensive Marx-ist treatment of the woman question on the American scene" to build a similar society (Epstein 93–94).

While the Party advanced its analysis of the intersections of gender, race, and class oppression, sexuality remained a taboo subject. Even though several women involved in Party leadership were lesbians (including Elizabeth Gurley Flynn, Grace Hutchins, and Rebecca Pitts), they remained closeted within the Party.[5] Some lesbians found refuge in the Mattachine Society, a gay and lesbian liberation group founded by several Party members and led by Harry Hay. But this group, too, fell prey to McCarthyism, as the group's leaders resigned in fear that their Communist affiliations would destroy the organization. A conservative leadership took over and eradicated the radicalism of its founding leaders. Women's involvement had been limited anyway, as the society's agenda professed to include lesbians but did not address their needs as women (Meyer, "Gay" 258–60).

In 1955, eight women founded the Daughters of Bilitis in order to provide lesbians with an organization that would address their needs in the struggle for social change. In 1956, the group began publishing *The Ladder*. While it was originally intended as the monthly newsletter for the organization, it quickly became in demand throughout the United States. At the time, no other publications existed specifically for lesbians, and *The Ladder* provided a space where lesbians could see their own interests reflected. Fearful of political repercussions, many of the writers wrote under pseudonyms, including Lorraine Hansberry (Damon i–iii.). Using only her initials, Hansberry published two letters in *The Ladder* on the connections between sexuality and economic oppression. To the best of my knowledge, her letters represent the limited body of publications by Party women on sexuality. Although the Party made great strides in its approach to the Woman Question, its position on sexuality was a glaring blind spot.

Otherwise, though, the Communist Party made great efforts to lend its official support for its new approach to women's issues. In order to encourage discussion among its members, the Party began offering courses dealing with the Woman Question at the Jefferson School of Social Science, a Marxist educational center located in New York City. Established in 1943, the school offered hundreds of courses and sponsored lectures, forums, and workshops. In June 1949, the school sponsored an all-day conference, "Marxism and the Woman Question," which attracted over six hundred men and women. In the fall term of that year, the school began offering a regular course on the Woman Question, which addressed issues such as women's oppression, marriage and family relationships, responses to male supremacy, and the triply oppressed status of black and Puerto Rican women. Over the next several years, the school offered courses by Claudia Jones, Myra Page, Elizabeth Gurley Flynn, Alice Childress, and Lorraine Hansberry. In 1953, Eleanor Flexner (aka Irene Epstein) and Doxey Wilkerson compiled materials from these various classes and published *Questions and Answers on the Woman Question*, a twenty-page pamphlet that included a special section on Negro women. This pamphlet most likely drew on Jones's classes on black women's history and political involvement (Weigand 90–91). Flexner also relied on Betty Friedan's *UE Fights for Women Workers* pamphlet in her own classes (Horowitz, *Betty* 1).

The Party presses also provided a forum for educating members on the Woman Question. In 1950, the *Worker* introduced a new women's page, sponsored by the National Women's Commission and edited by Peggy Dennis. Dennis shared editorial responsibility with Jones, and under their leadership, the page became a fertile ground for debate and discussion of women's political involvement. They abandoned the page's prior emphasis on cooking and fashion advice and expanded the letters section to increase debate on the Woman Question. Whereas, previously, the *Worker* had used examples of militant Soviet women to challenge the domestic ideology in the United States, Jones and Dennis shifted the focus to emphasize stories of women's activism in the United States. They encouraged submissions by black women writers and activists (Hill 88). While women's issues were by no means the top priority in the *Worker*, Dennis and Jones helped ensure that they were given serious consideration.

In Harlem, Paul Robeson's militant black newspaper *Freedom* (published monthly from 1951 to 1955) provided a forum for addressing the triple oppression of black women. Under the leadership of general manager Thelma Dale, the newspaper addressed women's roles in labor, antiracist, and anticolonial struggles; celebrated female artists; and challenged negative cultural images of black women. An article appearing in one of the first issues underscored the paper's commitment to black women's issues: "The sufferings and struggles of Negro women throughout America's history have made them a vast reservoir of power which is still only beginning to find expression. When the power of Negro women is fully realized and correctly utilized, it will add great strength to mankind's fight to bring freedom, equal rights, peace and progress to the whole earth" (J. Wilson 7). Dale, who had been active in the NNC in the 1930s, was at that time a labor organizer and activist in the Harlem community, and her activism was directly linked to her efforts to make black women's issues a priority at *Freedom*. She gave women on staff free reign to integrate a feminist point of view with the paper's international socialist perspective.

Alice Childress's regular "Mildred" columns addressed domestic worker issues, and many of her columns responded to ideas or events in the rest of that month's issue, explaining the ideas, making them accessible to readers, and often suggesting ways that readers could take action. Additionally, Lorraine Hansberry reported on women's participation in revolutionary colonial struggles, linking women's antiracist activism in the United States to women's roles in colonial struggles worldwide.

The Party's cultural journal also worked to include coverage of women's issues. Although the staff and the editorial board of *Masses and Mainstream* were predominantly male, Barbara Giles, Shirley Graham (Du Bois), and Meridel Le Sueur were among the original contributing editors. Submissions by women included the reportage of Le Sueur and Anna Louis Strong, short stories by Sanora Babb, book reviews by Giles and Graham, and the poetry of Naomi Replanski, Eve Merriam, and Lorraine Hansberry. International contributors included Australian novelist Dora Brittles, Polish writer Zofia Nalkowska, and Israeli literary critic Ruth Livinth.

Several members of the editorial staff had strong records of advocating on behalf of black women's political participation and contributing to the Party's ef-forts to reclaim black women's history, and *Masses and Mainstream* took serious-ly the project of chronicling the activism and leadership of black women histori-cal figures. Samuel Sillen, the journal's editor, published *Women against Slavery* (1955), a collection of sketches of women leaders in the abolitionist movement. Associate editor Herbert Aptheker included several essays on black women in his "Negro history" books and published "The Negro Woman" in *Masses and Main-stream* (1949). Lloyd L. Brown (whose 1951 novel *Iron City*, while not focusing on black women, presents them as strong and militant partners in the struggle) was also on the editorial board, as was Shirley Graham, who wrote a biography of poet and ex-slave Phillis Wheatley. Alice Childress's one-act drama *Florence* (1950) and Martha Dodd's short story "Maria" (1950), both of which deal with the political awakening of working-class black women, appeared together in the March 1950 issue.

At a time when government propaganda and the mainstream culture indus-try were championing images of women as tied to the home, women writers on the Left were turning to the past to find evidence that the emerging domestic ideology was a new development. To show that this domestic ideology had never been a reality for many American women, they drew on examples of women's participation in resistance movements throughout US history, including the abolitionist, labor, and women's suffrage movements, even though the field of women's history had yet to be established. Gerda Lerner and Eve Merriam's *The Singing of Women*, a dramatic revue of women's activism from colonial times to the present, produced off-Broadway in 1951, is an example of efforts to show connections to other feminist moments in US history. Friedan's 1953 pamphlet *Women Fight for a Better Life! UE Picture Story of Women's Role in American History* celebrates the contributions that black, working-class, and activist women have made to struggles against racial and economic exploitation. *Masses and Main-stream* would often publish special creative works honoring women's historical activism, such as Eve Merriam's poem "Spring Cleaning" (1952), which praises the multiple battles that women have fought to increase their rights in American society, and Ettore Rella's poem "These Treasures in the Earth" (1952), which celebrates women's contributions to the labor movement.

The Left's line on the connections between domestic ideology and fascism challenged the conventions of femininity rampant during the postwar era and provided an opening for women to discuss the ideological and cultural aspects of women's oppression. Some literary texts challenge dominant standards of beauty and efforts to keep women submissive to men, while others take issue with the expectation that women be defined by their roles as wives and mothers. Other writers challenge the notion that women do not belong in the political realm, and still others champion images of women as militant activists, fighting to challenge fascism and oppression, both in the United States and internationally. The fictional representations of women and relationships in the pages that follow draw upon the issues raised within the independent women's organizations that evolved during this era, as well as in the pages of the Party presses. Left feminist culture from this era must be read not only against the backdrop of McCarthyism but also within the context of the issues raised in the Party presses. In the chapters that follow, I will explore the often-reciprocal relationship between the Left feminist ideas being discussed and debated in the Party presses and the culture these ideas spawned.

CHAPTER 2

Fighting Fascism at Home and Abroad

The Cold War Exile of Martha Dodd

> Modern Day America with its policy of internal and external oppression, its
> brutal exploitation and calculated genocide has long been in the making; and
> also in the making have been the resistance, protest and fury which are now
> gathering forces in the country.
> —Martha Dodd, biographical note for *The Searching Light*

In her obituary of writer Martha Dodd, Katrina vanden Heuvel writes, "In death,
as in life, Martha [Dodd] Stern will be best remembered for her indictment on
unproven espionage charges"; and, indeed, little has been written on Dodd that
is not about her numerous affairs and her alleged espionage involvement with
the Soviet Union. In the 1930s, she supposedly had affairs with high-level French
and German officials, including Rudolf Diels, the head of the Gestapo, and writers Thomas Wolfe and Carl Sandburg, and was seduced into spying for the Soviet
Union after falling in love with the Soviet diplomat Boris Vinogradov (Brysac
141, 153–57). Historian Allen Weinstein and former KGB agent Alexander Vassiliev describe her as a "courtesan, agent, and student of communism," willing to
sleep with "leading Nazis and other notables" in order to assist the Soviets (53,
50). While the evidence in recent works of Dodd's espionage and promiscuity
would seem to be damning, the accuracy of the materials on which these works
are based is questionable, and thus Dodd's reputation continues to be the subject of much debate, even after her death in 1990.[1]

My purpose in this chapter is neither to refute nor defend the charges against
Dodd. Rather, I seek to examine her literary career, which has been obscured
by the controversy surrounding her.[2] A committed antifascist, Dodd wrote two
novels to call attention to the dangers of fascist control: *Sowing the Wind* (1945),
about the rise of fascism in Germany, and *The Searching Light* (1955), about the
rise of McCarthyism in the United States. In these two novels, as well as her
short story "Maria," she uses female activists to challenge some of the conventions about femininity in the immediate postwar era. Dodd's work is distinc-
tive among novels from this period; she presents women not simply as domestic
goddesses or morality police but as actors in their own right. This chapter establishes the connections between her writings and an emergent Left feminism
during World War II and the postwar era.

Dodd was involved in the antifascist resistance movement connected to the

Communist Party in the United States, and many of Dodd's writings reflect the changes in the Party's approach to the "Woman Question" during World War II and the postwar era. Much of Dodd's work reflects a Left feminist perspective on the connections between domestic ideology and fascism. In her two novels, she showed how fascism oppressed women and offered images of activist women to counter what she saw as the fascist domestic ideology of both Germany and the United States. *Sowing the Wind* shows the damaging effects of fascism on German women and highlights the role of women in antifascist resistance movements; *The Searching Light* makes connections between fascism and political repression in the United States during the McCarthy era. In *The Searching Light*, Dodd portrays resistance not as un-American but as the means necessary to achieve American ideals. The novel suggests that women best exemplified the American spirit when they participated in the struggle against fascism rather than remaining confined to the home and teaching children Cold War values. In both novels, Dodd contrasts the domesticity and self-sacrifice of older generations of women with the freedom and rebellion of youth; young women serve not only as the consciences of other characters but also as the chief representatives of resistance and liberation.

Both novels also reflect the ways in which women activists were marginalized, as Dodd puts white men at the center of both novels. However, these men falter and fail precisely because they do not listen to the more radical voices of the white female activists, who insist on the need for coalitions with other antifascist, antiracist, and labor groups. In her shorter works, too, Dodd explores some of the obstacles that hindered women's activism. Her 1950 short story "Maria" describes the development of political consciousness in a black, working-class Cuban woman who learns to break out of her shell of passivity and to challenge the class, race, and gender roles she is expected to fulfill. While maintaining a focus on the importance of women's activism, these works of fiction further illuminate some of the tensions and obstacles faced by women on the Left in the postwar era.

Like some of her protagonists, Dodd took some time to achieve the conviction that a women's place was in the collective struggle against fascism. In order to understand her commitment to antifascist resistance, some understanding of her process of coming to political consciousness is necessary. Dodd was born on October 8, 1908, in Ashland, Virginia, but her family moved to Chicago shortly after her birth. Her father, William E. Dodd Sr., chaired the History Department at the University of Chicago. Dodd's father encouraged critical thinking and the exchange of free ideas both in the classroom and at home; Dodd writes that one of her father's main objectives and ideals was the "triumph of democracy in the modern world" ("Biography"). While her father did his best to instill the values of democracy in his children, Martha Dodd developed little concern for social problems.

As a young woman, Dodd worked as assistant literary editor for the *Chicago*

Tribune. While working for the *Tribune*, she began writing short stories, hoping to make the shift from literary critic to author. Robert Morss Lovett, a professor of English literature and composition at the University of Chicago, tried to make her see the impossibility of living and working in isolation from economic inequality and other forms of injustice. But these concerns, she writes, "only touched the surface" of her mind. Despite her respect for Lovett, she continued to believe that artists and writers should remain unaffected by society. And although she shared a close creative and personal relationship with socialist poet Carl Sandburg, he, too, failed to develop her social consciousness. She remembered, "He revealed the profoundest contempt for the aloof, the objective spirit," but she "fought against his ideas, reviled radicals and their ilk, and resented the emphasis that he put upon the simple man" (*Through* 6, 8). Dodd resisted these efforts to politicize her, holding fast to her belief that books and politics should not interfere with each other.[3]

The Great Depression, which forced many other writers and artists to rethink their relationship to society, also failed to radicalize Dodd. But she did not remain entirely unaffected by the poverty and labor strife around her. Shortly before moving to Germany, she witnessed a protest strike in which police officers clubbed and fired shots at unarmed workers. When she related the incident to her family, someone commented, "Well, well, you seem to have turned into a Bolshevik, standing up for those strikers so ardently." Dodd, however, refused to see her response as a political statement and wrote of the incident, "I resented being called a Bolshevik; I was merely sympathetic with people who had expressed their ideas bravely" (*Through* 6–7). Although she did not want to connect her sympathy for the strikers' plight to any larger sense of political responsibility, she was growing more aware that not all Americans enjoyed the freedom that she had been taught to value.

She also began to realize that American society did not allow women full equality. Ella Winter's *Red Virtue: Human Relations in the New Russia* (1933), which she was assigned to review for the *Tribune*, introduced her to the possibilities for women's economic and moral emancipation under socialism. As she had been taught that Russia oppressed "the freedom and initiative of the individual" and therefore could not be "anything but dangerous to the human soul in the long run," the argument that socialism could improve gender relations surprised her. But while the ideas presented in Winter's book clearly stimulated Dodd, she claims in her memoir that she was not willing, at that point in her life, to question her situation as a woman in the United States or to acknowledge flaws in American society (7–8).

Interestingly, Dodd's first published story, "Poet's Wife" (*Story* magazine, 1935), addresses women's lack of power in a cultural sphere inhabited and defined largely by men. In the story, Dodd contrasts the creativity of the male poet with the creative production of childbirth. The story focuses on a nameless woman married to a self-centered poet who abandons her and their young child. Clearly, this woman had been marginal to the life of the great poet. When the story opens, she stands facing the ocean, which "was even this moment hers without meaning" (1). The sea, like everything else in her life, has no meaning without him; she defines her existence solely through him.

The woman's memory of her initial meeting with the poet is one in which she has no voice and no agency: "She stood very still, vast silence winging through her. The gleaming scales of her past life seemed to fall away from her, lay scattering in bright apprehensive bits at her feet." His very presence has the power to take away everything in her life that mattered up until that point. He effectively erases her history or any sense of an independent self that she once had. His very presence gives the newly blank slate of her life meaning; he makes her feel "fresh and renewed" (3). Yet he does not acknowledge her in a similar fashion. Indeed, he treats her as an object to be viewed. As she stands at a distance from him, he *talks* to her brother, while he *notices* her. His failure to see her as a thinking individual continues as their relationship progresses, yet it does not seem to bother her. Instead, she is pleased by his appreciation of her beauty and is content to bask in the glow of his accomplishments.

After a time, however, she grows somewhat disillusioned with their relationship. When she first attempts to question the emptiness of their life together, he takes no offense at her comments. Instead, he grows more self-righteous, telling her, "I am a good provider, you do not have to sit in the rain, you have a dress on your back, there is food I get to put in your belly, you have my poetry." In comparing his poetry to food, clothing, and shelter, he tells her, in effect, that his poetry is one of the basic necessities in life, something without which she cannot live. But on this diet, she becomes, in her own words, "a pitiable creature." In order to maintain some semblance of self-respect, she reminds herself that she once had a meaningful life apart from him (4).

Her restlessness and anger build, to the point that she stands up to him for the first time. She tells him, "I demand, since I am your wife, and you are responsible for me, that you make money from your poetry since that is all you can do." In her boldness she is no longer small; she feels herself standing taller, her words more firm. The poet's reaction to this show of strength is to slap her, to exercise his physical power over her, as his creative capacities no longer seem to carry the weight they once did. After this episode, he begins to withdraw from her, as he lacks the ability to deal with her on an emotional level. In response, she exercises the one power in her possession that he cannot refuse to acknowledge: her ability to produce a child. When she sees him falter when she tells him she is pregnant, "she knew that she had triumphed. . . . [S]he thought he was hers at last" (4–5). Her power as a mother provides her with an ability to create that had once solely belonged to him, leading her to believe that the balance of control in their relationship has shifted.

After she announces her pregnancy, their relationship does change, although not in the ways that she had hoped. He abandons his writing and devotes his time and energy to her care. In order to nurture her creativity, he must abandon his own. However, once she has this power, he no longer desires her. He refuses to accept her ability to create. She continues to believe that the birth of their child will change him, that he will embrace the intimacy of family life for which she so longs. He does not share her pride in their daughter's birth, though. When she places the baby in his arms for the first time, "she [sees] no tearing emotion rend his calm, no hope or joy light his face. This accomplished birth was denied even the pride he gave to the finished creation of a poem" (6). He cannot share in the joy of the occasion, as he did not create it. He leaves her shortly thereafter, blaming her for the failure of their relationship and his diminished creative output.

Even after he is gone, the only creative status she desires is in connection to him. She believes that her life without him will have no meaning, that she will be just another woman, rather than a poet's wife. Yet if she remains in mourning for him, she retains a certain aura. She considers her marriage to him the greatest accomplishment in her life: "Having been his wife, that she could enlarge upon without personal accomplishment" (7). Dodd's descriptions of the wife make it clear that she disapproves of the wife's desire to build on her husband's reputation. Most of the adjectives she uses to describe her are diminutive or unflattering. She introduces the wife as she stands "dreary and small," watching the sunset and contemplating the emptiness of her life. Her unsympathetic portrayal of the poet's wife implies that she views the woman as a victim not of a male-dominated creative sphere but of her own passivity. The story ends unhappily; although the majority of the narrative consists of a series of flashbacks, the story closes by returning to the original image of the woman standing alone on the beach, thus accentuating her weakness and isolation.

"Poet's Wife" critiques this lack of appreciation for female power and creativity, and Dodd's negative portrayal of the poet's wife seems to suggest that women have a responsibility to work to change this situation. Yet while Dodd had an interest in women's issues even at this early stage of her literary career, she had no interest in working to transform gender relations, or to work for social change in any capacity. Dodd's political apathy changed in 1933, when Franklin Delano Roosevelt appointed her father ambassador to Germany and she decided to accompany her family to Berlin. In her 1939 memoir *Through Embassy Eyes*, written shortly after her return from Germany, she claims that she could not pass up the opportunity to experience German society as an ambassador's daughter and so she left her job at the *Tribune* and moved to Berlin with her family. However, she was also leaving behind what Shareen Brysac refers to as her "dark secret," a failed marriage to George Roberts, a New York banker (138).[4] When she first arrived in Germany, she was seduced by what she saw as the efficiency and success of the Nazi Party. However, she quickly recognized the brutality and insanity of the Nazi program. The numerous atrocities she witnessed and the suppression of free ideas clashed with the liberal ideals she had come to expect as a basic right in the United States and made her realize that she could not remain neutral. In an unpublished essay, Dodd later referred to Nazi Germany as her "political baptism of fire" ("Biographical"). During the four and a half years she spent living under Nazi power, she developed a profound awareness of and hatred for the destructiveness of fascism and became involved in the pro-Soviet antifascist resistance movement, as she saw the Soviet Union as an important ally in the war against Hitler.

Upon her return to the United States in the winter of 1937, she became involved in the growing antifascist movement connected to the American Communist Party. In an interview for the New York *World Telegram*, she made one of her first public statements on the subject:

> When I went to Berlin with my father four and a half years ago I wasn't much concerned about Fascism. I had been the assistant literary editor of the Chicago *Tribune* for two years, and was mainly interested in writing short stories. . . . I thought that writing was the be all and end all. . . . I saw a lot of Fascism, and I made up my mind about it. I am opposed to Fascism in all the forms it takes. . . . Cultural life has disintegrated in Germany. There are no good writers left, except those in the concentration camps. The good ones are in exile (Press).

In publicly professing her opposition to fascism, she asserted that good literature could not survive in an atmosphere of political repression, making the connection between culture and politics that she theorized and practiced for the remainder of her life. Rather than being a writer completely removed from society, she now wanted to be a writer who changed it.

In 1938, Dodd married Alfred K. Stern, a public housing expert who had recently been appointed to New York City mayor Fiorello H. La Guardia's Committee on Property Improvement. While most accounts of Dodd's alleged espionage include accounts of her numerous affairs, letters in her correspondence files suggest that in Stern, she found a partner who shared her political commitments. The two were involved in numerous Left causes, including public housing, health care, racial justice, labor rights, and antifascist struggles, and were active in the American Labor Party, a pro-Communist party on whose ticket Stern ran (unsuccessfully) for Congress in 1940.[5]

Shortly after returning to the United States, Dodd became involved in the American Writers' Congress, a conference established in 1935 by the Communist Party with the goal of creating a revolutionary literature in America. While the original Writers' Congress focused on the role of the worker, the political agenda in the second and third congresses had shifted to the battle against fascism.[6] Although male authors dominated the first two congresses, women began to play a more active role by the third. In 1939, Dodd attended the third congress and was elected to the national board, along with Lillian Hellman, Genevieve Taggard, and six other women and seventeen men. Writer and literary critic Dorothy Parker and union activist-songwriter Aunt Molly Jackson also took part in the proceedings. At the fourth congress in 1941, Dodd was reelected to the national board, along with Taggard, Joy Davidman, Muriel Draper, Eleanor Flexner, Ruth McKenney, Myra Page, Tess Slessinger, and six other women, plus twenty-three men ("Women" 4; Wald, *Exiles* 259).

Dodd's first novel, *Sowing the Wind*, contributes to the project of using literature in the service of antifascist resistance. It also reflects Communist Party women's position on connections between domestic ideology and fascism. *Sowing the Wind* tells a chilling tale of the rise of Nazi power and its corrupting influence on Eric Landt, a brash young pilot and respected war hero with a deep and unflagging love for his country.[7] The novel centers on Landt's transformation from a good-hearted individual to a degenerate and inhuman Nazi general, and Dodd uses him to show the appeal of fascism and its power to seduce even those who question it. Even though Landt disapproves of many Nazi actions, he is willing to work with the Nazis because he believes that they have the best interests of Germany at heart. Hitler, as Dodd represents him in the novel, possesses the shrewd ability to play on Landt's intense patriotism, and Landt proves unable to resist. Although he makes a few efforts to challenge some of the more repressive aspects of the regime, he lacks the courage to renounce all ties to Germany or to abandon the wealth and power he enjoys as a Nazi officer. As the story progresses, he becomes more and more unable to recognize the evils of National Socialism, and he grows blind to the consequences of his own actions.

Dodd based her representations of fascist violence and repression on her own experiences living in Germany. At the same time, her treatment of women's oppression reflects a Left feminist perspective on the relationship between sexism and fascism. *Sowing the Wind* shows German women's role in resistance to the Nazi regime, despite a national ideology that strove to keep them powerless. While Dodd places a man at the center of her novel, she gives the strongest voice of antifascist resistance to a woman. While the novel focuses primarily on Landt's moral decline under fascism, the main female character, Lina, attempts to get him involved in fighting against Nazi power. At the beginning of the novel, Lina acts as Landt's conscience, cautioning him against further involvement with the Nazis and forcing him to see the corrupting and reprehensible actions that he would rather overlook. Lina is an avowed feminist and anti-Nazi, and Dodd presents her as a foil to Landt's blind patriotism and need for power. Landt is drawn to her from their first meeting, and for a while she provides him with the courage to rebel against Nazi influence, giving him the strength to resist that he does not have on his own. She provides the sole voice of critique throughout the novel, pointing out injustices and encouraging Landt to take action, yet she feels powerless to act herself. When Landt challenges Lina to work with him to oppose Nazi policy, she responds by asking, "What can a woman do today in Germany" (127)?

Lina's recognition of women's lack of power in Nazi society leads her to believe that women cannot resist the roles thrust upon them. The few scenes between Gertrud and Wolfgang Von Richter, an aristocratic couple loyal to the Nazi regime, depict these roles with brutal clarity. Gertrud tells herself after Wolfgang insults her, "It was a woman's role . . . to accept the arrogance and abuse of her husband, to enjoy her subservience, to obey her husband's whim to the last letter. . . . [I]t was good, it was instinctive and a part of National Socialist ideology to recognize the superiority of men" (46). According to this ideology, women are valued for their femininity, their skill in maintaining the home, and their ability to bear children for the Third Reich. Lina, who wears her hair short and thrives on intellectual exchange, manages to maintain a sense of independence, but she obviously feels thwarted by such an environment. Gertrud, who accepts this role unquestioningly, eventually sees the emptiness of her life. She commits suicide, believing she has no other options for escape.

While women, as Lina acknowledges, have almost no power under National Socialism, they nonetheless represent the few possibilities for resistance in the book. Lina eventually comes to see the cowardice in her failure to act, recognizing that she had "tried to evade responsibility on the grounds of being a woman," and joins the German underground (130). Her courageous actions for the underground movement demonstrate the importance of women's refusing to accept their position in a fascist society. Her actions with the underground mirror many of the stories told in the pages of the *Daily Worker* during the war, stories that featured the heroism of female antifascist fighters in the Soviet Union and Germany.

Dodd also shows how individual groups of women found ways to resist fascism outside of the organized resistance movement. One of the most powerful scenes in the novel depicts a group of working women waiting in line at a butter shop. Frustrated by their lack of access to basic necessities, such as food and clothing, they begin criticizing the Nazi regime. After one woman is arrested for speaking out too loudly, each of the remaining women places her hand on the shoulder of the woman in front of her in line, forming "a curious living chain of strength, pity and resolution" (150). Their silent gesture of defiance affirms both their solidarity and their refusal to submit to repression. In standing together, they create, at least for a few moments, a space in which Nazi power cannot touch them.

Dodd suggests that no successful resistance movement evolved in Germany because of a failure to unite these isolated pockets of resistance. The Nazis' multiple forms of oppression—their suppression of working-class agency, their commitment to maintaining racial purity, their treatment of women, and their use of homophobic, xenophobic, and anti-Communist rhetoric to divide the opposition—worked effectively to consolidate their power. Lina, in refusing her disenfranchised place in society and rebelling with other victimized groups, acts courageously, as do the women at the butter shop, but the actions of a few courageous souls are insufficient to challenge the breadth of Nazi power. The novel's tragic ending demonstrates the devastating consequences of failing to work with others in the fight against fascism. Landt succumbs completely to fascism; he deteriorates into a fat, miserable drunk who perpetuates the violence he once condemned. Lina's actions in the underground, without the numbers of a mass resistance movement to support them, result in her life sentence in a concentration camp.

Dodd's novel was widely reviewed and highly acclaimed. It received high praise from Thomas Mann and other exiled German writers for its effectiveness at capturing the repression of Nazi Germany. But in her 1945 review of *Sowing the Wind*, Eleanor Roosevelt expresses uneasiness with the novel's ending. She writes, "It left me with a sense of emptiness and hopelessness"; and, indeed, the novel's final image of "an enormous white tomb erected over the ravished land" (Dodd, *Searching* 311) contributes to a feeling of the pervasive destructiveness of the Nazi regime and its ability to annihilate the spirit of a people. Read in the context of Dodd's other work, though, the novel can be seen less as a statement that fascism will always triumph and more of a warning against the danger that results when a critical mass of people accept its horror. If Lina and the women at the butter shop had connections to a broader movement, Dodd suggests, they might have been able to do more in the battle against fascism.

Within a few years of *The Searching Light*'s publication, Dodd saw a frighteningly repressive climate emerging in the United States. In her writings, she often made connections between the fascism she witnessed in Nazi Germany and the political repression in the United States during the McCarthy era. As she wrote in 1958 for a German edition of *Sowing the Wind*, "The reader will certainly recognize that the plot and the events described in the novel, are of an appalling verisimilitude today. He has only to read his morning newspaper to know that similar occurrences are taking place" (postscript to German edition). The similarities she saw between the repression of the McCarthy era and the fascism she witnessed in Nazi Germany haunted her, especially as she herself became a victim of McCarthyite repression.

Throughout the 1940s, Dodd and her husband were accused of being Soviet agents, harassed by the FBI, and vilified by the media. Due to their outspoken antifascist politics (and their generous contributions to the American Communist Party), she and Stern suffered vicious character attacks and custody threats regarding their adopted son, Bobby. By 1953, the persecution had become so intense that she and Stern, along with Bobby, fled to Mexico City in order to escape the slanderous attacks against them. Sources close to the Sterns believe that the couple was also trying to escape FBI threats regarding their son. According to several friends and relatives, the FBI contacted Bobby's birth mother and forced her to sue the Sterns for custody of the child on the grounds that their Communist involvement made them unfit parents. Rather than risk losing their son, they left the country.[8] Several years later, Dodd claimed that they were attacked for two reasons: "First, because we were, and are, committed anti-fascists and learned a long time ago that the end of war and exploitation of man can only be achieved with the destruction of big capital, and, second, because our names and our case could have been very useful to further the hysteria of fear and other ends of the cold war in the Unites States" (postscript to German edition). In 1957, a federal grand jury indicted Dodd and Stern in absentia on espionage charges after Boris Morros, a former Hollywood producer and US counter-spy, identified Dodd as a Soviet agent in his House Un-American Activities Committee (HUAC) testimony. His testimony clearly established both Sterns "as part of the Soviet apparatus"; he claimed he met them through a Soviet official and that Stern advanced him $130,000 for a business to be used as "an espionage cover" ("Morros" 1, 12). Morros, who was later proven to be a spy for both the Soviet Union and the United States, was not considered to be a credible witness by many journalists of the time, and the Sterns denied all charges. In a press release issued in September 1957, they decried Morros's accusations as "fantastic inventions" and described their persecution as a "vicious technique Morros and the agencies of the US government and Committees of Congress are employing to try to destroy or silence those people who dare to dissent" (Dodd and Stern 2). Despite their repeated assertions of innocence, they were forced to alter their lives irrevocably in order to escape the continued attacks against them. They never returned to the United States, spending the rest of their lives in Mexico, Cuba, and Prague.

In 1951, Dodd began working on her second novel, *The Searching Light*, as a response to the insidious attacks against her. She intended for her novel to educate people about the dangers of McCarthyism and the necessity of collective resistance to it. The novel tells the story of the battle by Professor John Minot and several of his colleagues against the imposition of a faculty loyalty oath. While Dodd portrays the fight against the loyalty oath as primarily a white, middle-class male struggle, she again makes women the heroes of the novel. While the female characters might lurk at the edges of the novel's central plot, they are by no means spectators. Instead, their voices provide the strongest call for collective resistance in the book, and they encourage the men to develop an awareness of the need for coalitions with other victimized groups.

Given her reputation and the novel's subject matter, she had difficulty finding a publisher. Harcourt, Brace, and Company, which had published *Sowing the Wind* and *Through Embassy Eyes*, refused *The Searching Light*, even though these first two books were widely reviewed and very well received.[9] Citadel Press accepted the novel for publication in 1955, and it was eventually published in the United States, England, Italy, Czechoslovakia, Poland, Germany, and the Soviet Union. It was generally favorably received, both in Left and mainstream presses, as a novel possessing both political relevance and aesthetic value.[10] Within the Left, writers and activists such as W.E.B. Du Bois, Albert Maltz, and Annette Rubinstein recognized the novel's value for resistance movements, and it was circulated at Left book clubs.[11] Albert Einstein, who publicly defended academic freedom, wrote Dodd that he had read her novel "with great interest" as it "shed light on the whole morbid and fantastic process of which we are witnesses." He went on to say, "Your work merits, in my opinion, the attention of all reasonable people who are interested in the social problems of our day" (Einstein).

The novel takes place over the course of an academic year at the fictional Penfield University, a small, liberal arts college nestled in the Appalachian Mountains of Virginia. In a letter to a friend, Dodd claimed she based Penfield on "a composite of universities leaning heavily on the University of California" (Letter to D. N. Pritt). In 1949, as part of their campaign to eliminate Communism in education, the University of California Regents began requiring all faculty members to sign loyalty oaths stating that they were not members of the Communist Party. Over thirty professors refused to sign and were subsequently fired, even though none of them were—or had ever been—Party members. Following in California's footsteps, other universities, both public and private, began pressuring faculty members to sign similar oaths. The imposition of these oaths was generally the first step toward the regents' asserting control over classroom content (Schrecker, *No* 116).

Dodd traces the repression on Penfield's campus from a supposed effort to eradicate Communism to a thorough surveillance of speech and classroom content. The witch hunt at Penfield begins under the pretense of eradicating Communism on campus in order to protect the value of American education, but the persecution shifts gradually to those who refuse to sign the oath. Most of the non-signers fought to integrate Penfield's campus, were involved in labor strikes, supported immigrant rights, and protested against Franco's regime in Spain. As Minot tells his wife, Julia, "They're not after Communists here, they're after nonconformists of any shade of political opinion." And Blackwell, Penfield's president, affirms Minot's suspicions. Referring to the non-signers, he says, "They've been active in all the campus ruckuses and they cooperate not only with their colleagues but with the students! This university needs a real house cleaning" (*Searching* 167, 94). Like other writers on the Left, Dodd represents the crusade against Communism as a means of establishing complete control over educational and cultural institutions, rather than as a strategy that was necessary to protect the United States from a violent takeover. She tried to show that the events on which she based her novel were not isolated or unique incidents. As Minot's daughter, Lucy, points out to her father, "There's nothing special about the case at Penfield. It's the trend all over the country" (119).[12]

Dodd portrays the crusade against Communism as un-American, equating the climate of repression that develops on Penfield's campus with the early stages of fascist control. She saw this climate as building toward a level of intolerance and surveillance similar to the one she experienced in Nazi Germany, and her book can be seen as a warning against allowing this repression to remain unchecked. Origano, an Italian artist whose father was killed for refusing to sign a loyalty oath, fears that the United States is headed on a similar path as the Italian fascist regime. He claims, "My youth was ruined by oaths. I thought there'd be some security in America, in a democracy" (133, 135). Eventually, he commits suicide rather than go through the repression he experienced in Italy. As Origano tells his colleagues when they doubt the loyalty oath will be imposed, "It happened in Italy, it happened in Germany, why shouldn't it happen here?" (21). In looking beyond the repressive acts to examine the effects of this repression on American culture, *The Searching Light* helped expose the hypocrisy of McCarthyism.[13]

But as important as her denunciation of the Red Scare's effect on men's lives and work is Dodd's critique of the ways in which the domestic ideology of the era limited women. As in *Sowing the Wind*, this novel's treatment of domestic ideology was in keeping with the Party's postwar position on the connections between fascism and male chauvinism. While, during the war, Communist women provided alternate images of antifascist fighters in other countries, in the postwar era they championed images of American women activists. Likewise, Dodd constructs two strong female activists who challenge the domestic ideology embodied in some of the other women in the story.

In many ways, Minot's wife, Julia, exemplifies that domestic ideology. She has a "strong sense of her duty as a wife" and has sacrificed her life for her family, but Dodd presents her life as rather empty. Dodd afflicts Julia with a serious heart condition, suggesting that this kind of life is deathly for women. Even with this illness, Julia has trouble stepping outside her role of wife and mother. When Lucy tells her she should not work so hard to do things for her, Julia replies by asking, "What would my life be worth if I couldn't do for my family?" (172, 11, 35). She defines herself through serving her husband and daughter; her identity exists only within the domestic sphere. As John's wife, she views his success as her own. She helps edit and type John's books and articles, providing support for his work but not producing anything on her own. She has no independent identity in the outside world.

As the book progresses, however, Julia comes to see the emptiness of her life and wishes she had "learned some profession, or developed a youthful talent which could have filled the empty years when her family grew beyond her." She regrets some of her decisions, regrets sacrificing herself for her marriage and family: "Instead of an ailing and querulous woman she would have been a wife whom John could lean on, respecting her equal courage." By end of book, she wants "to live bravely and well, for myself too." After this realization, Dodd lets her begin to get well, suggesting that only through breaking free from these roles can women be healthy (61, 259, 330).

Throughout the book, Julia tries to encourage her daughter to fulfill her proper role as a woman, and she worries that Lucy will be so wrapped up in her career that she will fail to get married. Lucy, however, rejects her mother's values, telling Julia, "I like my life—but maybe it won't be just like yours" (29–30, 14). And the life Lucy chooses is one in which she will create politically meaningful art in the tradition of 1930s artists and the Mexican muralists.[14] Furthermore, as an outsider to the events at Penfield—she lives and works in New York City—Lucy is able to see the oath in a wider context. She continually reminds her father and the other professors that Penfield's situation is not unique and warns them that they cannot see the situation on their campus as separate from other instances of McCarthyism. While her mother suffers for her adherence to the domestic ideology, Lucy's rejection of these values enables her to become a valuable part of the professors' struggle. As Origano tells her shortly before he kills himself, she is "the best of America" (257).

Like Lucy, Alice Aiken calls attention to the need for the professors to look at their situation beyond Penfield's campus. Alice, a young student activist, warns the professors of the dangers of intellectual isolation, urging them to see their struggle as linked to labor and antiracism struggles. In many ways, hers is the most courageous and uncompromising voice in the book. Dodd's choice to give this voice to a woman was clearly intentional; Alice has a twin brother who shares her politics but rarely speaks. Throughout the novel, Alice holds Minot and the other professors accountable for their compromises and their failure to act. She helps organize student protests, and she remains loyal to the professors' cause even after the other students abandon it. The novel's final scene takes place at the graduation ceremony, which occurs after all the professors have signed the oath or been fired. At the ceremony, Alice refuses her diploma, and in an impassioned speech, she announces that Penfield has corrupted American education and avows her allegiance to the fired professors. Even though she acts alone, the importance of her act is recognized by the audience. The book ends with these lines: "The clapping started at first slowly, strong but not boisterous. Then a dozen more people joined in, and gradually the applause scattered through the hall . . ." (345). By ending her novel with a round of applause for the female activist and then trailing off with an ellipsis, Dodd leaves open possibilities for other people to join Alice in her struggle.

As in *Sowing the Wind*, Dodd highlights the necessity of collective resistance. The professors lose their battle against the oath, Dodd implies, because of their failure to form coalitions with other groups victimized by the crusade against

Communism. In a postscript written for the Czech edition of the novel, Dodd compares Penfield's climate to the fascism she witnessed in Nazi Germany:

> Unfortunately, a great number of Americans, like a great number of Germans be-
> fore them under Hitler, plagued by anxieties about their economic security and
> their future in this atomic age, have been psychologically prepared to blame any
> minority, like the Communists, the Jews or the Negroes for their sterile uncertain
> life and therefore fall easy prey to the vicious propaganda of the hate-mongers who
> are now in control of national life.

In linking anticommunism to racism, economic exploitation, and gender in-equality, Dodd shows how they are all elements of fascist control. Thus, both books stand as a call to form coalitions between these exploited groups as the only effective response to political repression and incipient fascism.

While both of Dodd's novels use female radicals who encourage the male characters to become more politically active, these works do not address the process by which women themselves become politically conscious. She explores this process in her short story "Maria," published in *Masses and Mainstream* in 1950. The story describes the development of class and race consciousness in a black, working-class Cuban woman whose husband organizes the cane workers on a sugar plantation. It appeared in *Masses and Mainstream* in the same issue as Alice Childress's one-act play *Florence*, which deals with the political awaken-ing of a black, working-class woman in the American South, suggesting that the Communist Party wanted to raise awareness of the obstacles to women becom-ing politically active.

When the story begins, Maria's husband, José, has recently been killed by the plantation overseer for his organizing work. At first, Maria's actions are limited to grieving over her husband's death and worrying about their young child, Jo-sefina. Even these actions are always guided by what her husband would have wanted. After his death, she moves to live with her sister's family in the city because his fellow workers tell her that "José would have wanted her to go." Once in the city, she refuses to accept charity to feed her daughter because José "could not have endured the sight of his wife begging with his daughter looking on" (21, 20). Although she desires to provide a better life for Josefina, she adheres to his wishes nonetheless. Her actions represent her lack of agency, her inability to make decisions for herself.

At this point in the story, she does not understand why José would have wanted her to refuse charity. She does not yet have the awareness of the Cuban class structure that keeps people like herself in a permanent underclass. When people offer her coins, she regrets her inability to support her daughter on her own and thinks about how hard it was "to be proud when you had nothing, ab-solutely nothing." José, she knows, "would have risen angrily from the bench and cursed the givers," but "she was not like that." She lacks the angry pride that her husband recognizes as a necessity for someone in their class position. José repeatedly told her "that to have no anger or to have anger and keep it inside, was a bad thing," but she clings to her gentle ways (20).

As a male worker, José had recourse to his male comrades in the sugar fields, whom he taught to "help one another like brothers" (21). And they respond by standing in solidarity after José's death. But Maria has no such "sisters" on whom to rely, and thus she has difficulty learning the value of solidarity and resistance. Through her role as a mother, though, she gains the courage to stand up to an attempt to remind her of her place in society. Not wanting Josefina to be subject to humiliation, she refuses to accept the offer of a grapefruit for her child, rolled across the street and into the gutter by a woman who clearly reeks of class privilege. Maria recognizes the woman, in her silk stockings and fur coat, as "that 'certain kind' of *blanco*, predatory and rich, the Cuban of the sugar plantation." She cannot accept a gesture of charity from a woman who represents the power of the sugar plantation responsible for her husband's death. When the woman yells at Josefina to pick it up, Maria, who up until that moment believed herself incapable of hatred, decides to act:

> With the dignity of a slow gathering but inevitable rebellion Maria stood up slowly, gave the woman a long hateful look, cleared her throat as loud as she could and spat hard and full at the golden fruit in the gutter, and then kicked it savagely across the street again. Trembling with rage she sat down and moved close to the child on the bench. (23–24)

For the first time, she recognizes that hatred against those who have power over her can be empowering.

And her action has direct results; the woman becomes frightened and flees the scene. In standing her ground, Maria retains her dignity and gains the satisfaction of triumphing over someone more powerful. Additionally, she gains the respect of others. The fruit vendor clasps his hands over his head in a sign of victory, telling her, "*Bien, bien*, my friend. Well done! That is the way, all right" (24). But more importantly, she learns the power of anger and resistance. While she does not take on the role of male revolutionary leader that José played, she finds her own way of resisting the Cuban power structure. While at the beginning of the story, Maria believed that she was defined by her role as wife and mother, by the end of the story she has learned that women can and do play a role in resisting race and class oppression.

Although Dodd's work clearly reflects what today would be referred to as feminist consciousness, like many female activists in the 1930s, '40s, and '50s, she shied away from using the term "feminist." Yet, although she preferred to be known for her antifascist work, she did not want to ignore the issue of women's oppression; indeed, she saw the fight to end women's oppression as a central part of the battle against fascism. In her laudatory memoir of radical writer Agnes Smedley, she explains how Smedley saw possibilities for transforming gender relations through socialism. This 1960 essay, entitled "Daughter of Earth" (or "*Hija de la Tierra*," as it was titled when published in the Cuban *El Mundo*), provides some insight into Dodd's own Left feminist ideals. In it Dodd discusses the lessons Smedley's work provides in regards to the possibilities that socialism offered for women:

> Agnes Smedley was wrongly called a "feminist." What she really wanted and fought for all her life was the revolutionary power of the working class, and full legal, sexual and economic equality for women. . . . [She was convinced that] an honest and equal relationship between men and women would be possible only after revolution, and even then would be slow in evolving. "Property relationships must change, and also the habits of men!" (2–3)

Like Smedley and other women writers on the Left, Dodd saw the struggle against fascism and racial and economic exploitation as linked to the struggle for gender emancipation. Both women made sure that women's issues did not get silenced on behalf of any greater struggle. In a 1981 letter to a friend, Dodd referred to herself as "a woman liberationist . . . from the old days," acknowledging the importance that she placed on women's issues (Letter to David Klopfer).

Dodd believed that women could not enjoy full equality under fascism or capitalism, and she often wrote about the possibilities that socialism offered for women. After leaving the United States, she continued to maintain connections to Communist organizations in China, Prague, the Soviet Union, and the United States. While living in Mexico, Dodd was part of an exile community of blacklisted artists, including several members of the Hollywood Ten. Her papers include correspondence with Jack Lawson, who wrote about sexist images of women in films in "Degradation of Women," a section in *Film in the Battle of Ideas*, his 1953 study of Marxist film criticism. She also exchanged letters with Paul Jarrico, the producer of *Salt of the Earth*, and the actress Gale Sondergaard (wife of *Salt* director Herbert Biberman), who performed a one-woman Marxist-feminist show in the 1950s. Many of these people participated in discussion groups and seminars that focused on the connections between gender, race, and class oppression, and many of them were working to incorporate representations of women's activism into their cultural works. Given her efforts to address women's activism in her writings, Dodd more than likely would have been part of such discussions.[15]

Many of Dodd's essays from the late 1950s and 1960s address the benefits of living in a socialist society, such as attention to child welfare, affordable food and housing, efficient public transportation, shared community facilities, and readily available health care. These essays (published primarily in foreign periodicals) are similar to ones published in the *Daily Worker* during this time, comparing women's experiences in socialist societies to women living under capitalism. Likewise, Dodd described the services available to improve women's lives in socialist societies. In articles such as "Hoyerswerda: Socialist New Town" (1960), she interviewed women in the German Democratic Republic about the advantages that socialism provided for women, including facilities and support to "relieve woman of household drudgery, and the excessive hours and worries connected with childcare" ("Hoyerswerda" 108). In "Waiting at Poprad, CSSR" (1961), she describes the childcare services a small town in Slovakia had established for women who lived and work in the town. Although useful historical documents, these later writings presented an idealized and uncritical view of the libratory possibilities socialism offered for women and do not reflect the contradictions and obstacles that her earlier work illuminates. These nonfiction works reflect an uncritical belief that socialism would relieve women of their domestic duties, yet her fiction shows that achieving equality for women was not so easy.

Taken together, Dodd's cultural work provides a glimpse of some of the contradictions and tensions for women on the Left as they fought courageously in the battle against fascism, both home and abroad. Sadly, the FBI harassment damaged her career as both an activist and a writer. In a 1959 letter to *Mainstream* editor Charles Humboldt, written shortly after she and her husband moved to Prague, Dodd wrote, "There is no way of conveying the excitement a writer feels over here, at last to write and be published!" (Letter to Charles Humboldt). In the rest of her letter, she describes the vibrant cultural community there and the prospects it provided for artists and writers. While she felt energized by this group, other letters reflect a desire to return to the United States. Although she built ties to resistance movements in Prague, China, Cuba, Mexico, and the Soviet Union, her writing was her only means of remaining connected with the Left in the United States. Purged from literary and feminist history, Dodd's work addresses ideals of alliance-building and consciousness-raising that remain relevant to an understanding of feminist movements, both in the United States and internationally.

CHAPTER 3

"In Her Full Courage and Dignity"

Alice Childress and the Struggle against Black Women's Triple
Oppression

In 1949, in response to an argument with Sidney Poitier and several other actors
who claimed that only "life and death" issues like lynching mattered in racial
protest plays, Alice Childress wrote *Florence* (Abramson 189). Written overnight,
this one-act drama expresses Childress's frustration with the prevailing notion
within the Harlem Left that only black male issues were central to the racial
struggle. At a time when black women within the Left were pushing the Communist Party to reconsider its position on the Woman Question, Childress helped
to educate the Left on what Claudia Jones referred to as the "special problems of
Negro women" ("End" 51) by creating a play that showed the effects of segregation, limited job opportunities, and racial violence on working-class black wom-
en. In *Florence* and several of her 1950s writings, *Trouble in Mind* and her Mildred
columns (originally published in *Freedom* and later collected in *Like One of the
Family: Conversations from a Domestic's Life*), Childress explained these "special
problems" to men and white women within the Harlem Left and encouraged
working-class black women's radical activism, despite efforts to contain political
resistance during the McCarthy era.

While her 1950s writings advocate a militant stance, Childress does not assume that such a position will come easily or naturally to most black women. Indeed, she shows a profound sensitivity to and understanding of their fears of the
consequences of radical activism. All three works, while emphasizing the value of
resistance, anticipate the hesitancy some readers might feel. In *Florence*, Mama
Whitney wavers between wanting to support her daughter Florence's efforts to
break racial barriers and worrying that Florence will be better off if she does
not cause trouble. While Mama struggles to do the right thing by her daughter,
by the play's end, she decides that she cannot be complicit in perpetuating her
daughter's oppression. In *Trouble in Mind*, Wiletta Mayer, a middle-aged black
actress, undergoes a similar struggle to Mama's. She fears that challenging the
racist representations in the Broadway play in which she has a part will jeopar-
dize her acting career. She eventually decides that she cannot remain silent and
stands up to the play's racist director. While both Mama and Wiletta struggle
with the decision whether to take a stand against racial injustice, Mildred, the
domestic worker in Childress's "Conversations from Life" column, is unapolo-

getic about her resistance from the beginning. Childress uses Mildred's friend, Marge, a fellow domestic, to voice potential concerns with Mildred's militancy, but Mildred addresses Marge's fears while still affirming the value of activism. Through these works, Childress explains the necessity of resistance to her readers and encourages solidarity with others seeking similar goals. In the process, her characters take men and white women to task for their chauvinism, forcing them to reevaluate their own racist and sexist assumptions and challenging cultural stereotypes about black women.

Until recently, existing biographical and critical studies of Childress made no reference to her connections to the Harlem Left in the 1940s and '50s. But her Left commitment during this time cannot be disputed: she organized in pro-Communist women's organizations and labor unions, participated in protests against McCarthyism, contributed to Left journals such as *Freedom* and *Masses and Mainstream*, and recruited actors and young people into the Left. Her FBI file paints a picture of an activist solidly rooted in the Left. Her file is well documented with press clippings and organizational reports that show her involvement in a multitude of Left-sponsored activities. From organizing May Day parades to leading songs at Party meetings, to staging cultural events for the Congress of American Women and the Civil Rights Congress, to teaching dramatic workshops at the Jefferson School, Childress was intimately involved in using culture in the service of the struggle.

Yet despite her active Left involvement, feminist critics have tended to overlook the ways in which Childress's cultural work was inextricably bound with her political work. Most critical approaches to Childress's work address her feminism but omit her Left roots. Gayle Austin, for example, argues in "Alice Childress: Black Woman Playwright as Feminist Critic" that Childress was incorporating feminist criticism into her work long before it emerged as an identifiable field in the 1970s (53–62). Elizabeth Brown-Guillory agrees that Childress was ahead of her time; she describes Childress as "the mother" of black women's playwriting and claims that her "pioneering spirit" helped engender black feminist theater in the 1970s and 1980s (*Their* 46). While Austin and Brown-Guillory rightly acknowledge Childress's influence on later generations of black feminist writers and the significance of her work to black feminist criticism, they fail to link her feminist criticism to her participation in a Left feminist community in the 1940s and 1950s, a community that included Lorraine Hansberry, Claudia Jones, Thelma Dale, Yvonne Gregory, Shirley Graham Du Bois, and other women who were working to make black women's issues a priority within the Left. In discussing Childress's cultural work as if she emerged out of a vacuum, these works overlook the source of development of her feminist ideas.

Likewise, Trudier Harris argues that Mildred challenges stereotypical views of 1950s black domestic workers. In her introduction to the 1986 Beacon Press reprint, Harris writes that she became determined to track down a copy of the collection after hearing about it from Childress in 1978. Harris, who had several friends and family members who worked as domestics, writes, "Childress's voice in *Like One of the Family* was different from most I had heard. She dared to test assumptions about the expected." Harris claims her discovery of *Like One of the Family* inspired her to write *From Mammies to Militants: Domestics in Black American Literature*, a book-length study on cultural representations of black domestics (Introduction xiv–xv). In this study, she discusses the ways that Mildred broke new ground by refusing to let her employers define her or keep her in her place. She claims that Mildred's "moral strength, independence, assertiveness, and positive conception of herself must have served to inspire many domestics to dare to recognize such things in themselves." Harris goes on to say that, for these workers, "the possibility of breaking out of the maid's confining space, even as an abstract possibility, was liberating" (*From Mammies* 130). But what Harris overlooks is that Mildred was not offering abstract hope to exploited domestic workers; she provided concrete guidelines for maids of all races to work together to change their material conditions. While Harris sees Mildred as a transition to the militant maids of the 1960s, the original publication of Childress's Mildred columns in *Freedom* indicates that Childress was encouraging militancy among her black working-class readers in the 1950s.[1] While Harris, of course, mentions the stories' publication in *Freedom*, she does not address the newspaper's Left politics. By not attending to the Childress's Left involvement, Harris underestimates the value and utility of Childress's column to her readers.

In addition to overlooking the Left component of Childress's McCarthy-era writings, most critics fail to take into account the conservative political climate of the age. At a time when many black writers were abandoning protest in favor of integration into mainstream society and culture, Childress provided an unabashedly militant stance against black women's oppression. In 1959, she participated in the first conference of Negro writers, sponsored by the American Society of African Culture (AMSAC). One participant's speech described the shift in black literature to an inward focus on black life, rather than on conflict with external forces. Many black writers, he said, were striving for "universality" rather than blackness, and protest was either played down or avoided (Arthur Davis 37–38). While many writers at the conference spoke of protest writing with what Loften Mitchell described as a "condescending attitude," Childress's panel (which Mitchell chaired) agreed that the black protest tradition should be sustained. As Childress pointed out, though, black writers were rewarded for avoiding racial conflict and ignored when they did not (Mitchell, "Negro" 55–60). The published proceedings of the AMSAC conference underscore her point: the more militant speeches—including Childress's own—were excluded in favor of the more conservative voices. As Mary Helen Washington has argued, the published collection is the perfect document of Cold War containment, as some of the most radical voices are suppressed (lecture).

Despite the political and cultural efforts to contain progressive activism throughout the 1950s, Childress refused to be silenced. She continued to work for racial justice and social change and used her plays and Mildred columns to encourage protest and political commitment. However, like the AMSAC proceedings, literary history has suppressed the Left element in Childress's works. A notable exception to this erasure of Childress's Left past is Mary Helen Washington's "Alice Childress, Lorraine Hansberry, and Claudia Jones: Black Women Write the Popular Front" (2003), which argues that all of Childress's writings emerged from her involvement with the Left in the 1940s and 1950s. In this piece, Washington seeks to resituate Childress within African American literary history and to acknowledge the role the Left played in shaping African American cultural production in the 1950s. In so doing, she builds on the pioneering work of James Smethurst, Alan Wald, William J. Maxwell, Bill V. Mullen, and others. Another notable exception is Kevin Gaines, who argues that the "black feminist foresight" in Childress's work can be traced to "a radical black culture of internationalism" in the postwar era (296, 294). This chapter, then, works to build on these works by reading Childress's 1950s writings in the context of her Left activism and her connection to a Left feminist community. I argue for the significance of Childress's work to the development of black feminist literature and criticism by looking at the ways that she developed her ideas as part of a cadre of Left women who fought to create an alternative to the dehumanizing stereotypes of black women in film and on television.

In her essay "A Candle in the Gale Wind," Childress attributes her class consciousness and political commitment to her family history and her own experiences growing up in a working-class household (111).[2] Childress was born in 1916 in Charleston, South Carolina. As the great-granddaughter of a former slave, she was the descendent of a long line of women raised in extreme poverty. Her parents separated when she was five years old, and she moved to Harlem to live with her maternal grandmother, Eliza Campbell White. Although White had never gone beyond the fifth grade, she continued to educate herself, and she instilled this responsibility for learning in Childress, exposing her granddaughter to art, history, poetry, and community events. She also encouraged her to respect and appreciate her relationship to her community. Through witnessing the struggles faced by her grandmother and the other working-class black women in her neighborhood, Childress came to value their strength and resiliency. Given her early awareness of social inequality and her desire to remain rooted in her community, Childress's gravitation to Left circles in Harlem is not surprising.

While Childress was growing up, Harlem served as the center of radical black cultural and political activity. African Americans were actively involved in the Communist Party during the Great Depression, and the Party worked closely with the National Negro Congress and the Scottsboro defense movement.[3] As black soldiers returned from World War II, the issue of racial justice took on a whole new sense of urgency. Having just defeated fascism and white supremacy abroad, many black soldiers had high expectations that America would become more racially tolerant. The message they got, though, was that conditions would be the same as before the war. Many blacks refused to accept the status quo and became determined to bring about social justice. The Party provided a way for them to do so. Even if they were not members, many blacks joined organizations that worked closely with the Party, which had a strong base in the Harlem community.

Childress came to the Left by way of the theater. Her frustration with racial prejudice and the stereotypical roles offered to black women in mainstream American theater led her to help form the American Negro Theatre (ANT). Founded in 1939 by Abram Hill and Frederick O'Neal, the ANT sought to create an experimental and interracial people's theater in the Harlem community, one that would provide realistic images of black life (Pitts 2).[4] In a speech given at the 1945 Conference of the Arts, Sciences, and Professions, Hill defined the ANT's goal: "to revolutionize Negro participation in the theater—to project men and women on the stage as men and women rather than as exotic distortions" (J. Jones 14). Throughout the 1940s, the ANT turned increasingly leftward. Over the years, many actors associated with the Left came through the ANT ranks, including Sidney Poitier, Harry Belafonte, Ruby Dee, and Ossie Davis. For many of these actors, the Harlem theater scene served an activist as well as a cultural purpose. As Belafonte remembers, "We made it our business to become part of any force that was speaking out against this inhumane cruelty." And Davis recalls, "We were determined to force the issue of justice for everybody on the public consciousness—and the total theatrical community seemed to be caught up in that" (*Scandalize*). O'Neal and many other ANT members were later summoned before HUAC for their Left activities. Many were blacklisted and unable to find work.

As the ANT folded in the late 1940s, Childress became increasingly involved with the Committee for the Negro in the Arts (CNA), which served as the cultural division of the Civil Rights Congress. The Civil Rights Congress was formed shortly after World War II as a result of the merger of several labor and antiracist groups connected to the Communist Party (Horne, "Civil" 134–35). Founded in 1947 after these various organizations merged, the CNA sponsored cultural productions that furthered a Left agenda. Like the ANT, the CNA was an interracial organization that sought to create a permanent black theater in Harlem and "to help erase the persisting racial stereotype and to create employment for Negroes in the various art fields" (*Just a Little*). Childress served on the Finance Committee of the Civil Rights Congress and as the chair of the Production Committee for the CNA. The CNA sponsored the production of several of her early plays, including *Florence* and *Gold through the Trees* (Federal Bureau of Investigation).

Through her work with the CNA, Childress strove to make black culture and history accessible to the Harlem community, and she worked to create institutions that would promote black culture as well as a Left agenda. Along with actress Clarice Taylor, Childress started a community theater in Harlem. John Barone, the owner of the Club Baron bar and grill, offered them free use of space at his bar. Paul Robeson donated $500 and lent his support, appearing at fundraisers and bringing people to performances. The Club Baron theater lasted for several years (Duberman 703). Childress also served on the board of directors and the Cultural Board of the New Playwrights, Incorporated, a dramatic company that produced Marxist and pro-labor plays. Childress starred in the New Playwrights production of *Candy Store* (1951), a play that focused on a strike against a chain drugstore in a New York neighborhood. Several performances of this play were staged as benefits for the United Electrical Workers Union (a Communist-led union) and for the Civil Rights Congress (Federal Bureau of Investigation). She also taught dramatic workshops and led creative forums on black art and culture at the Jefferson School of Social Science, a Marxist educational center in Manhattan, and at the Frederick Douglass Educational Center, an offshoot of the Jefferson School in Harlem. Additionally, she directed cultural activities at Camp Unity, an interracial pro-Communist resort in Upstate New York.[5]

While she worked to make black culture and history priorities within the Left, she fought to ensure that black women's history did not get excluded. She found strong support for this project within the Left, as the Party had recently begun to emphasize the importance of black women's history, largely due to the influence of Claudia Jones's 1949 *Political Affairs* article, "An End to the Neglect of the Problems of the Negro Woman!" In this article, Jones asserted that black women have been "the real active forces—the organizers and workers—in all the institutions and organizations of the Negro people" (57). She went to great lengths to show the ways that black women have been historically powerful leaders in struggles for racial justice. Childress responded to Jones's "challenge to progressive cultural workers to write and sing of the Negro woman in her full courage and dignity" ("End" 64) by emphasizing black women's historical contributions in the yearly Negro History Week celebrations that she helped organize and in her plays and Mildred columns. Her 1952 play *Gold through the Trees* depicted women's participation in black liberation movements over the course of several centuries, linking struggles in South Africa, the West Indies, and the United States. This play, which was produced by the CNA, was the first play written by a black woman to be produced professionally on the American stage. It received glowing reviews from Lorraine Hansberry in *Freedom* and from Lloyd L. Brown in *Masses and Mainstream*.[6] Several Mildred columns show Mildred working to educate young people about Harriet Tubman and Sojourner Truth. Mildred also informs people of the role that domestic workers and black mothers have played in supporting future generations. And Childress's use of music by a female blues singer in *Trouble in Mind* connects Wiletta's struggle in that play to the collective struggle of black women.

Childress found support for her promotion of black women's culture in a number of Communist-led women's organizations. She worked with the Congress of American Women (CAW), an interracial group that emphasized grassroots organizing. The CAW worked seriously to recruit black and working-class women around issues such as women's equality in the workplace, job training for women, childcare, racial discrimination, and national health care. The Harlem branch was led by Claudia Jones and Thelma Dale, both of whom were active in the Party. Childress also helped to start the Sojourners for Truth and Justice, a national coalition of black female activists working to force the federal government to take action against racial violence. Formed in September 1951, this organization brought together trade union and Communist women, domestic and factory workers, PTA members and students. Childress's work with these organizations brought her in contact with a cadre of women working to address black women's oppression.

Childress also found support for her ideas in the Left feminist community at *Freedom*, Paul Robeson's militant black newspaper, which openly supported black women's issues and integrated a feminist dimension into its international socialist perspective. At *Freedom*, Childress worked closely with general manager Thelma Dale, a labor organizer and founding member of the CAW, and with Lorraine Hansberry, whose articles frequently incorporated ideas drawn from Claudia Jones's "An End to the Neglect of the Problems of the Negro Woman!" In addition to raising funds and soliciting contributions for the paper, Childress wrote a regular column, "Conversations from Life," which introduced readers to Mildred, the feisty domestic later anthologized in *Like One of the Family*. Childress's column addressed domestic workers' issues and offered suggestions for black women on ways to respond to topics raised in each month's issue. She often asserted the need to unionize domestic workers, an idea for which Dale and Claudia Jones argued in *Political Affairs* and the *Worker*. Many of her columns can be traced directly to Jones's article, especially in regards to black women's triple oppression, black women's labor history, and the need to challenge stereotypical representations of black women. Her *Freedom* columns were a way of making the Party's theory on the Woman Question accessible to men and women, both within the Left and within the Harlem community. Often, she used Mildred to critique racism and sexism within the Left, forcing men and white women to question their own chauvinism.

Childress's desire to educate men and white women within the Left about black women's struggles led her to write *Florence*, a play that showed that violence against black men was not the only problem facing the black community. *Florence* helped launch Childress's career as a respected playwright within Left cultural circles and established her as an important spokesperson on black women's issues. The play first appeared in August 1950 as part of a CAW-sponsored educational event.[7] A month later, it appeared as part of *Just a Little Simple*, Childress's adaptation of Langston Hughes's *Simple Speaks His Mind* and the first theatrical production of the CNA. This musical review, which showcased "an array of exciting talent in song, comedy, drama and dance," opened in September 1950 and ran at the Club Baron Theatre and the Philadelphia Council of the Arts Sciences and Professions (*Just a Little*). In October 1950, *Masses and Mainstream* published *Florence*, further demonstrating its acceptance in Left circles. Although generally overlooked by the mainstream press, Childress's work was gaining recognition as important within the Left cultural realm.

As a critique of the Left's shortcomings on gender issues, *Florence* provided a subtle reminder that black women suffered from racial violence and injustice differently from black men. The play centers on the struggles of the title character, Florence, whose husband "got killed at voting time." Rather than making this implied lynching the focus of the story, though, Childress gives it minimal attention. Instead, she prioritizes Florence's struggle for survival after racial violence claims her husband, thus showing that the effects of lynching extend beyond the immediate male victim; wives, mothers, and children suffer as well. Florence refuses to accept her husband's death passively; she continues to challenge racial barriers and rejects the limited job options available to her as a black woman. After her husband's death, she moves to Harlem to become an actress, unwilling to stay in the South, where racial barriers and limited job opportunities keep black women from transcending their position. As her mother puts it, Florence just "don't feel right 'bout down here." But she finds that the North does not provide many more opportunities. Other than the occasional role as a maid, she has had trouble finding acting work and can barely meet expenses. With so few options available to her, she cannot easily escape the working class, and her struggle illustrates the ways that both cultural stereotypes and material conditions keep black women in their place (Childress, *Florence* 45, 36).

Although the play revolves around Florence's struggle, she never actually appears onstage. Instead, the other characters discuss her problems and suggest solutions. Through these characters, Childress shows an awareness of her audience's potential fears of challenging racial barriers. As the play opens, Florence's Mama waits for a train to New York; she plans to bring back Florence, who has written home to ask for money. The play's single act takes place in this railroad station in a small southern town. The stage, which is divided into "white" and "colored" sides, provides a visual map of Jim Crow laws, thus situating the play socially, politically, and geographically. A railing physically separates the two main characters—one white, one black—and Childress presents them in direct contrast to one another, both racially and class-wise. Mrs. Carter, a well-to-do white woman, enters covered in furs and carrying costly luggage, while Mama has her cardboard suitcase and shoebox lunch. While Mama talks respectfully to the porter and engages him in friendly conversation, Mrs. Carter talks down to him, calling the fifty-year-old man "Boy" and ordering him about as if he were her servant (38). This setting establishes expectations that blacks and whites are consigned to certain roles and acknowledges the segregation laws keeping blacks in their place.

Childress depicts Florence's sister, Marge, as the voice of the emerging Cold War containment culture and domestic ideology. Marge does not think blacks (especially black women) should challenge the status quo; she wants Florence to realize her place. As she tells Mama, "She got notions a Negro woman don't need." Florence, she thinks, is acting "white" by trying to become an actress, when clearly, as Marge recognizes, "Them folks ain't gonna let her be no actress." Marge has had a problem with Florence's "attitude" even before she moved to New York; Florence's history of fighting for jobs traditionally denied to blacks has always troubled her. While Marge does not "feel right" about living in the Jim Crow South either, she feels it is foolish to try to change things. "There's things we can't do," she tells Mama, "cause they ain't gonna let us." Furthermore, she feels that Florence is neglecting her responsibilities as a mother (and there-fore as a good woman) because she has left her young son behind for Marge to raise. She wants Mama to force Florence to return home, face her responsibili-ties to her son, and accept her role in life. Trying anything else, she believes, is futile (35–36).

Mama, on the other hand, is reluctant to bring Florence home. Throughout the play she wavers between wanting to support Florence's acting career and rec-ognizing the obstacles that Marge voices, a conflict she expresses to the porter when he asks her about the purpose of her trip. "I'm bringing Florence . . . I'm visiting Florence," she tells him, indicating her uncertainty as to what she will (and should) do. While Marge argues that Florence should know her place and stop acting "white," Mama recognizes that Florence is not alone in her efforts to fight against Jim Crow. "Others besides Florence been talkin' about their rights," she tells Marge (37, 36). She is torn between accepting and challenging the status quo. Through Marge and Mama, Childress allows her readers (or the play's view-ers) to work through their own fears and ambivalence. Mama's conflict shows a sensitivity to the difficulties black women face in trying to challenge their triply oppressed status.

Through Mrs. Carter, Childress provides a critique of white people who talk about racial equality but are not willing to see blacks outside of certain roles or stereotypes. Around the time that Childress wrote *Florence*, Claudia Jones had made a similar critique, calling on "white women progressives, and particularly Communists," to abandon their chauvinist attitudes toward black women and "to fight consciously against all manifestations of white chauvinism" ("End" 60). Mrs. Carter fancies herself a supporter of "Negro" issues, but Childress makes her appear foolish, uninformed, and unaware of both her class and her racial privilege. Mrs. Carter first strikes up a conversation with Mama by complaining about her problems, which involve her brother's bad reviews of his novel. She assumes Mama will understand why she is so troubled, yet she shows no awareness that Mama's problems—lynching, poverty, segregation, a daughter in financial trouble—are far more severe than bad reviews. Her brother's novel centers on a tragic mulatto who kills herself because she cannot accept that she has black blood. Mrs. Carter tells Mama that the suicide "was inevitable," believing that the character's knowledge of her blackness would be enough to drive her to suicide (41). The story agitates Mama, and she tells Mrs. Carter that she knows several light-skinned people who lead normal lives. These real-life examples confuse Mrs. Carter; she cannot seem to grasp that anyone who looked white could feel anything but shame at knowing they were black. Although she professes to feel compassion for blacks' situation, she still sees blackness as indicative of a lesser humanity. And the subject is, for her, merely one for discussion, anyway, rather than a lived reality for many black people.

While Mrs. Carter adamantly tries to prove her good intentions to Mama, she has little knowledge of the material realities of racial oppression. Her lack of understanding frustrates Mama, who tries to disengage herself from the conversation. But Mrs. Carter takes offense at Mama's withdrawal, and she tries to establish her antiracist credentials in an effort to redeem herself in Mama's eyes. Her brother, she claims, really "knows the Negro," while she herself has "eaten with Negroes" and recently gave a thousand dollars to a Negro college scholarship fund (42). Mama shows little interest in these acts of generosity, and Mrs. Carter cannot understand why these "close" ties to the black community do not impress Mama. In showing this tension and lack of understanding between Mama and Mrs. Carter, Childress deftly illustrates how the white woman's racial awareness is not based on real-life experiences or a desire to change material conditions for black people.

Instead of listening to Mama or trying to learn from her experiences, Mrs. Carter reverts to stereotypical beliefs about black women. As the conversation shifts to Florence, Mama learns that Mrs. Carter is an actress herself. She asks the white woman for her help, believing Mrs. Carter might be able to use her contacts to find Florence work. And Mrs. Carter readily agrees; she offers to arrange a job for Florence as a maid for a theater friend. In her mind, black women cannot be actresses; they can only be a part of the theater world by working for white actresses. Despite all her claims that she is sympathetic to black causes, she is unable to see black women outside of her limited worldview. She acts out one of the examples of chauvinistic behavior that Jones refers to in her article as "paternalistic surprise when it is learned that Negroes are professional people," as well as "the reverse practice of inquiring of Negro women professionals whether 'someone in the family' would like to take a job as a domestic worker" ("End" 61–62). Through Mrs. Carter, Childress illustrates the damage done by these attitudes and provides a challenge to both white men and women within the Party to examine their own chauvinism.

And through Mama, Childress provides a model for black women to stand up to white chauvinism. Mrs. Carter offends her to such an extent that she cannot let the white woman's assumptions go unchecked. Her anger is apparent when she grabs Mrs. Carter's wrist and tells her she better return to the other side of the railing. Mrs. Carter clearly does not grasp the implications or consequences of segregation policies. She refers to Jim Crow laws as "silly" but has no knowledge of their effect on people. Mama, on the other hand, knows the consequences all too well. She quickly drops the white woman's wrist, commenting, "I mustn't hurt you, must I." While Mrs. Carter excuses herself to the restroom, Mama tears up the piece of paper with the woman's name and telephone number and puts a check in an envelope to mail to Florence. She tells the porter, "She can be anything in the world she wants to be! That's right. Marge can't make her run back, Mrs. Carter can't make her turn back." Mama finally takes decisive action after recognizing that she does not want to be complicit in allowing either white people's stereotypes or her own fears to keep Florence down. Her note to Florence (enclosed with the check) says, "Keep trying" (46–47).

Through Florence, Mama, and Marge, Childress illustrates the specific struggles that black women face and encourages them to fight for their rights. While Mama hesitates to challenge the racial barriers for black women, she eventually emerges as a resistant character, challenging both Mrs. Carter's white chauvinism and Marge's acceptance of the status quo. By the end of play, Mama realizes that she must join in the struggle if she wants to make a more just and decent world for her daughter. Although the porter tells her, "Don't you fret none. Life is too short," Mama replies, "Oh, I'm gonna fret plenty!" She indicates that she will continue to fight for racial equality because the consequences of remaining silent are worse (47). Childress sends a message to black women that if they remain passive, accepting segregation, limited job opportunities, and the lynching of their husbands, then these various forms of racism will remain in place. The play also shows the need for solidarity, the need for black women to stand together and support each other in their struggles.

In *Florence*, Childress introduced themes never before seen onstage. Her commitment to radicalize the theater, however, went beyond the content of her plays. She also sought to transform working conditions for black actors and theater workers. In the early 1950s, she helped negotiate the first off-Broadway union contracts that recognized the Actors Equity Association and the Harlem Stage Hand Local (Jennings 6; Brown-Guillory, *Their* 29). Her union-organizing work addressed the need to consider black actors as workers exploited by mainstream theater, a theme she addressed in *Trouble in Mind*. First staged in 1955, this play showed the theater as a workplace for black actors.

While *Trouble in Mind* deals with labor in a way that *Florence* did not, the two plays address many similar issues: the stereotypical roles available for black actresses, the chauvinism of white people who profess to be antiracist, and the importance of black women's activism and collective resistance. This play revolves around the struggle of Wiletta, a middle-aged black actress, to challenge the racist representations in *Chaos in Belleville*, a Broadway play in which she has recently been cast. While the cast of this play-within-a-play is predominantly black, the writer, director, and financial backers are white; thus, the black actors have little say in the play's portrayal of racial politics. Although the actors have a union, they do not have much control over their working conditions; they are subject to the decisions of Manners, the white director. Even getting jelly donuts (which some cast members prefer) instead of Danish (which Manners prefers) results in controversy. Like *Florence*, the play seeks to encourage black women's activism and to force white viewers to question their own chauvinistic assumptions.

Like all of the other plays in which Wiletta has acted, *Chaos in Belleville* draws heavily on racial stereotypes. The black characters speak in an absurd dialect, black men are portrayed as ineffectual or as troublemakers, and black women are presented as obedient, servile, and passive. *Chaos in Belleville* revolves around a young black boy who incurs the wrath of the white townspeople by exercising his legal right to vote. Wiletta plays the boy's mother, who chastises her son for voting. In order to protect him from the lynch mob, she allows the wealthy white man for whom she works to put her son in jail. However, they are stopped on the way to the jail and the boy is lynched anyway. Wiletta feels her actions are unrealistic, and she tries to convince the director to change the script. In having Wiletta voice her concerns with her role, Childress draws on Claudia Jones's argument that the black woman "is the victim of the white chauvinist stereotype as to where her place should be. In the film, radio, and press, the Negro woman is not pictured in her real role." Jones defines this role throughout history as "the guardian, the protector of the Negro family" ("End" 55, 51). Wiletta feels her part in *Chaos in Belleville* is unrealistic precisely because it does not reflect her knowledge of black women's experiences. She believes that, as a mother, she would try to protect her son, rather than advise him to turn himself over to the white authorities when he is sure to be lynched.

While Wiletta and the other black actors recognize the racist ideology of *Chaos in Belleville*, the white director believes he is putting on a play that tackles "the explosive subject" of the "race situation" and will lead "to a clearer understanding" of "Negro rights" (221–22). As she did in *Florence*, Childress critiques the chauvinism of white people who ignore material differences—and thus conflict—between races by putting forth an idea of universality that effaces race. Manners and the white actors buy into this ideology: "I maintain there is only one race . . . the human race," Manners tells the cast (254). Likewise, Judy, a young white actress starring in her first play, asserts that "people are the same" and makes efforts throughout the play to socialize with the black cast members (217). However, although she claims, "I get so mad about this prejudice nonsense," she refuses to see her own complicity in maintaining racist stereotypes (230). She and Manners both believe that their assertion of equality absolves them from responsibility for fighting for equality.

As in *Florence*, Childress is sympathetic to her audience's hesitancy to challenge these chauvinistic attitudes. While Wiletta voices her concerns with the play, she also fears losing her job if she makes too much noise. Like Mama in *Florence*, she wavers between wanting to fight to change things and fearing the consequences of her actions. Throughout the play, Childress shows how Wiletta and the other black actors are members of the working class who have no control over the means of the play's production. Most of them live close to the poverty line, and they definitely view the play as a job. Throughout the play, they worry about living expenses and housing; losing their roles would leave them with no other means of economic survival. Their need to work takes precedence over challenging the play's stereotypes. They recognize that, in order to make sure they do not put themselves out of their jobs, they need to avoid appearing too angry. Millie and Wiletta complain about the dehumanizing roles in which they are cast repeatedly, but only to the other cast members. Millie describes her last role as being so embarrassing that she did not want her relatives to see the play. "All I did was shout 'Lord, have mercy!' for almost two hours every night," she exclaims (216). While they are tired of constantly wearing bandannas and baggy dresses and being named after flowers and jewels, they would never air their grievances to the director. They recognize that to do so would be fruitless. As Wiletta puts it, "It's the man's play, the man's money, and the man's theater, so what you gonna do?" (216). Wiletta and Millie express their frustration with these roles, yet they continue to accept the parts because they lack the resources to put on the kind of plays that they would like.

Wiletta's fear of losing her job makes her unwilling to try to change things. She still holds onto her dream of achieving the success, status, and glamour accorded to white actresses, and she is willing to accept the demeaning roles offered her in the hopes that she will eventually rise above them. Yet she holds no illusions about the likelihood of that happening, and she tries to warn others of the obstacles facing blacks in the theater world. When she first meets John Nevins, an up-and-coming young black actor, she tries to warn him that limited opportunities exist for a black man to get ahead in the theater. Her words fall on deaf ears though, as John believes he will be able to succeed because of his talent. He seems unaware of the obstacles facing blacks in the theater world, but he has not yet had to worry about paying the rent or finding an affordable place to live in a highly segregated housing market. Wiletta tries to explain to him that black actors have no say in their working conditions and are at management's whim. In order to maintain her tenuous foothold in the theater world, she has learned to be "Tommish" to white directors, and she tries to convince John that he should do the same. "You have to cater to these fools," she tells him. "Laugh! Laugh at everything they say, makes 'em feel superior. . . . White folks can't stand unhappy Negroes" (213). When John complains that he could not adopt this attitude, she lays it on the line: "You either do it and you stay or don't do it and get out" (213). She is willing to walk the line required by white directors if it will help her keep her job.

The years of remaining silent in the face of the racism and sexism of white theater finally take their toll, though, and Wiletta begins to speak out against the play's racist ideology, despite the fear that renders the rest of the cast speechless. Her attitude begins to change after a conversation with Sheldon, an elderly black character actor, in which he tells her, "You and me . . . we don't mind takin' low because we're trying to accomplish somethin." But Wiletta, who is beginning to see that she might never be able to accomplish anything, loses her patience, telling him, "I mind . . . I do mind . . . I mind . . . I mind" (235). At the end of act 1, she confides to Henry, the doorman, "Henry, I want to be an actress. . . . Where the hell do I come in? Every damn body pushin' me off the face of the earth! I want to be an actress. . . . [H]ell, I'm gonna be one, you hear me?" (237). As she pounds the table to emphasize her words, the act ends with the music of a woman blues singer. This music connects Wiletta's struggle to those of other black women, suggesting the need for solidarity.

Once Wiletta acknowledges her anger at having to compromise her integrity in order to accommodate the white culture industry, she begins voicing her criticisms to Manners (and not just to the other black cast members). Wiletta's problem with the script revolves around the scene in which her character advises her son to give himself to the white people for protection, an act that guarantees that he will be lynched. Wiletta, who had been troubled by the play from the beginning, finally articulates her problem with it to Manners. "The writer wants the damn white man to be the hero," she tells him. "And I'm the villain" (262). While Manners tries to tell the other cast members that she is just "confused," she does not bend to his attempts to silence her. "You don't want to hear," she tells Manners. "You are a prejudiced man, a prejudiced racist" (263). He refuses to accept this criticism, but Wiletta refuses to let him off the hook. She keeps pushing the issue, asking him repeatedly whether he would treat his own son the same way. He finally breaks and admits the truth: "What goes for my son doesn't necessarily go for yours!" (264). Although he has claimed all along that he sees no differences between races, he acknowledges here that profound differences exist. He storms out, and Wiletta and the other cast members recognize that she will surely be fired for provoking this outburst.

For Wiletta to take a stand is not easy, and her future in the cast is uncertain at the end of the play. The other black actors do not back her up, even though they are horrified at Manners's comments. Millie laments, "I know what's right but I need this job." John seems willing to support Millie, claiming, "We all ought to show some integrity," but in the end he leaves to go have "a calm chat" with the other cast members (266–67). If the cast had stood together—rather than leaving her to hang alone—they might have been able to save her job. Or perhaps they all would have been fired, but at least they would have made a statement about refusing to be treated a certain way, rather than surrendering their dignity and humanity. Although Wiletta does not regret standing up for her beliefs, this lack of collective action cripples the potential for social change throughout the play. In the end, Childress's play encourages viewers to follow Wiletta's lead and challenge white chauvinism and stereotypical representations of black women.

Not surprisingly, aspects of *Trouble in Mind* made white backers uncomfortable. The play ran at Greenwich Mews Theatre for ninety-one performances in 1955 and 1956. According to Childress's biographer La Vinia Delois Jennings, the play's producer "threatened to cancel the production if it did not end happily," and so Childress rewrote the ending (7). In the alternative version, Manners returns after his outburst and tells the cast that he wants to keep them all on but anyone who wants to quit can do so without fear of repercussion. When several cast members threaten to walk out, he has a change of heart and agrees to sit down and talk about how "to find a way to bring some splinter of truth to a prejudiced audience" (three-act version 3:26). Other aspects of the play, which indicate a deeper discontent on the part of the black cast members, are toned down or eliminated. For example, Wiletta's "I mind" speech (which shows that she does not just blindly accept the roles offered to her) is cut, as are other scenes that express the black actors' anger and unrest. This version of the play won a *Village Voice* Obie Award for best off-Broadway play, but Childress hated this ending and insisted on reinstating the original for any subsequent productions (Jennings 7).[8]

Trouble in Mind was optioned for Broadway but never staged because Childress refused to make the necessary script changes. In a 1964 interview with Doris E. Abramson, Childress confided that the producer wanted her to turn the play into a "heart-warming little story." When she refused to do so, the play was dropped, as the producer was not willing to take a chance on a play that would be financially risky (190). Ironically, Childress anticipated her play's fate in a scene between Wiletta and Manners in which Wiletta questions the play's stereotypes. "The American public is not ready to see you the way you want to be seen," he tells her. "One, they don't believe it, two, they don't want to believe it, and three, they're convinced they're superior. . . . Now you wise up and aim for the soft spot in that American heart, let 'em pity you, make 'em weep buckets" (264). While Manners wants a play that will allow white audiences to sympathize with the black characters, Wiletta wants a play that will force people to reconsider their preconceived notions about black people and act to challenge racist ideology. Childress wanted *Trouble in Mind* to be this kind of play.[9]

In both *Florence* and *Trouble in Mind*, Childress showed an understanding of black women's potential fears of militancy. In her Mildred columns, Childress presented something entirely new and different: a model of a strong black activist who showed readers how to stand up for themselves and demand justice. These columns focus on the daily battles of Mildred, a black domestic day worker. By allowing Mildred to relate her experiences in her own voice, Childress created an outspoken and militant working-class heroine who refuses to be subservient to the white women who hire her to cook, clean their homes, and look after their children. In the process, Mildred smashes stereotypical views of black domestic workers and provides an example of ways to stand up to the chauvinism of white employers. A few months before Childress's first column appeared in *Freedom*, Lorraine Hansberry addressed this issue in one of her own *Freedom* articles, critiquing the "distorted and degrading image" of the black woman as " a giggling, contented domestic, who . . . lives only to take care of her white employers and their children" ("Negroes" 7). Childress's various columns encourage strength, pride, and action rather than the passivity and submission expected of domestic workers.

The columns served the dual purpose of educating the Left about black women's issues and helping black women understand their place within the Left. Often, Childress used her column to help readers sort through ideas addressed in the rest of the issue and figure out the best way to respond to them. Most of her columns make accessible the discussions of black women's oppression taking place in *Political Affairs* and the *Worker*. After *Freedom* folded in 1955, Childress gathered her columns into a collection, which she published with Independence Publishers, a small Brooklyn publishing house, in 1956. Although the mainstream press and black journals otherwise ignored the collection, the book was widely circulated within the Left and reviewed in *Masses and Mainstream*.[10] The collection helped disseminate issues such domestic worker unions and black women's history to a wider audience.

For the black, working-class readers of *Freedom*, though, Mildred provided inspiration for exploited domestic workers who feared confronting their employers. Through her interactions with her white employers, Mildred shows the chauvinism of white people who profess to believe in racial equality but treat their black domestic workers condescendingly. In the column from which the collection takes its name, Mildred grows increasingly frustrated with one employer who raves to her friends about how much she and her husband "just love" Mildred because "she's *like* one of the family. . . . We don't think of her as a servant!" (Childress, *Like* 1). Mildred finally sits her down and informs her, "You think it is a compliment when you say, 'We don't think of her as a servant . . .' but after I have worked myself into a sweat cleaning the bathroom and the kitchen . . . making the beds . . . cooking the lunch . . . washing the dishes and ironing Carol's pinafores . . . I do not feel like no weekend houseguest" (3). After this speech, the employer apologizes profusely, and Mildred tells Marge that the rest of the family begins to treat her more respectfully. Through her example, Mildred empowers readers to stand up to their employers and shows the positive results that can occur; her boss even offers to consider the raise for which Mildred has the audacity to ask.

In a 1980 letter to Trudier Harris, Childress wrote that she received "floods of beautiful mail" from fellow domestics who not only approved of Mildred's actions but gave stories of their own protests (quoted in Harris, introduction xxvi). Harris describes Mildred's appeal as almost mythical:

> When maids read about Mildred, they must have felt something similar to what steel-driving men must have felt upon hearing stories of John Henry, or what slaves who worked from four in the morning until nine at night must have felt in response to tales about John Henry or Brer Rabbit getting out of work that the master or other animals required of them. (*From* 130)[11]

Indeed, Mildred's ability to speak out against exploitation and injustice—in a way that often changes the hearts and minds of those who hear her—often seems superhuman. But in providing such a model, Childress gave hope to her readers that they could borrow some of Mildred's wisdom and sassiness to stand up for themselves and to demand change and dignity.

Childress most likely used fellow pro-Communist writer Langston Hughes's Simple stories as a model for her columns. In Hughes's columns, which were serialized in the *Chicago Defender*, Simple shared his Harlem exploits with his friend Boyd.[12] Childress structured the columns as conversations between Mildred and her neighbor, Marge, a fellow domestic. In *From Mammies to Militants: Domestics in Black American Literature*, Harris writes that Marge allowed the domestic workers reading Childress's column to identify and express skepticism with Mildred's experiences. Harris writes, "Childress enables her audience to interact with Mildred in more personally satisfying ways than if they were mere readers; through Marge, they are allowed instead to be participants on the stage" (112). Mildred's conversations with Marge anticipate readers' concerns with adopting a similar militant stance. Whereas Mama in *Florence* and Wiletta in *Trouble in Mind* help readers learn the necessity of resistance, Mildred's confrontational and assertive style provides her readers with a model for action.

Many of her columns stress the importance not only of activism but also of finding support with other black women. In "All about My Job," Mildred establishes a kinship with her readers by letting them know that they can trust her because she does the same work as they do. She tells Marge, "I'm glad that you are my friend because everybody needs a friend but I guess I need one more than most people. . . . Well, in the first place I'm colored and in the second place I do housework for a livin' and so you can see that I don't need a third place because the first two ought to be enough reason for anybody to need a friend" (Childress, *Like* 33). This exchange with Marge works to highlight black women's triple oppression and to encourage solidarity with other domestic workers. Mildred lets her fellow domestic workers know that she shares their frustrations but does not remain silent in the face of her frustration. She voices her discontent, and she suggests that her readers should do the same.

One of the ways that Mildred encourages her readers to channel their discontent is through organizing a union to improve wages and working conditions. For several years, Thelma Dale had been campaigning for the unionization of domestic workers, speaking publicly on the issue and writing about it in the pages of *Political Affairs*. A 1949 *Worker* article, "Household Helpers Find It's Time to Help Themselves," describes the Party's strong support of the Domestic Workers' Union. Other *Worker* articles address the need for Social Security benefits for domestic workers. Mildred urges her fellow domestics to organize themselves, to recognize that "we are all servants and got a lot in common . . . and that's why folks need unions" (Childress, *Like* 63). And in "We Need a Union Too," she makes readers aware of the demands of the labor market. "Honey," she says to Marge. "I mean to tell you that we got a job that almost nobody wants" (140). Because they have this power and because they are exploited, Mildred recognizes that forming a union would help protect them. "Why shouldn't we have set hours and set pay just like bus drivers and other folks," she asks Marge. "Why shouldn't we have vacation pay and things like that?" (140).

In addition to encouraging domestic workers to organize, Mildred's pro-union stance pushes the labor movement to take domestic workers seriously. In *Political Affairs*, Claudia Jones had sharply criticized the labor movement's failure to organize domestic workers. She wrote, "One of the crassest manifestations of trade-union neglect of the problems of the Negro woman worker has been the failure, not only to fight against the relegation of the Negro woman to domestic and similar menial work, but to *organize* the domestic worker" ("End" 58). On several occasions, Mildred draws attention to the ways that US society relies on domestic labor:

> Domestic workers have done an awful lot of good things in this country besides clean up peoples' houses. We've taken care of our brothers and fathers and husbands when the factory gates and office desks and pretty near everything else was closed up to them. . . . Yes, there's many a doctor, many a lawyer, many a teacher, many a minister that got where they are 'cause somebody worked in the kitchen to put 'em there . . . [and] after freedom came, it was domestics that kept us from perishin' by the wayside . . . [and] it was our dollars and pennies that built many a school. (36–37)

While Mildred strongly advocates for the need to unionize, she also shows an awareness of what Jones referred to as "the real difficulties of organizing the domestic worker—such as the 'casual' nature of their employment, the difficulties of organizing day workers, the problem of organizing people who work in individual households, etc." Mildred acknowledges these difficulties, telling Marge on one occasion, "I guess it would be awful hard to get houseworkers together on account of them all workin' off separate-like in different homes, but it would sure be a big help" (140). But she soothes her readers' fears that their employers will simply hire non-union workers by stressing the value of collective action. "Well," she says when Marge raises the issue, "then the union calls out all the folks who work in that buildin', and we'll march up and down in front of that apartment house carryin' signs which will read, 'Miss So-and-so of Apartment 5B is unfair to organized houseworkers!' . . . The other folks in the buildin' will not like it, and they will also be annoyed 'cause their maids are out walkin' instead of upstairs doin' the work" (141). If they stick together, she tries to convince readers, they will win.

The Communist Party lent its support to the Domestic Workers' Union, and the woman's page of the *Worker* frequently featured stories of black women labor organizers and activists. Jones helped solicit such stories for the woman's page, and in several articles of her own, she described the active role that black women played in numerous political organizations. Jones also pointed out, though, that black women's contributions were not limited to specific movements:

> Historically, the Negro woman has been the guardian, the protector, of the Negro family. From the days of the slave traders down to the present, the Negro woman has had the responsibility of caring for the needs of the family, of militantly shielding it from the blows of Jim-Crow insults, of rearing children in an atmosphere of lynch terror, segregation, and police brutality, and of fighting for an education for the children. ("End" 51)

In several of her *Freedom* columns, Childress used Mildred's stories to educate readers about black women's unsung contributions to the survival of the black family.

In Childress's "The 'Many Others' In History," published in the 1952 black history month issue, Mildred tells Marge about a meeting she attended, at which the various speakers pay tribute to Harriet Tubman, Sojourner Truth, Frederick Douglass, Frances Harper, and John Brown. Mildred acknowledges that women are included in this list of historical figures, but she notes "that everybody would name a couple of folk and then add 'and many others.'" When Mildred has the chance to speak, she focuses her comments on these "many others," telling the

crowd about her grandmother, who raised seven children on her husband's earn-
ings as a mill worker:

> Every minute of grandma's life was a struggle. She never had a doctor except for
> "sickness unto death" and neighbor women helped bring her seven into this world.
> Sometimes she'd get down to the "nitty gritty" and have her back to the wall . . .
> all the trouble lined up facing her. What to do! What to do about . . . food . . . coats
> . . . shoes . . . sickness . . . death . . . underwear . . . sheets . . . towels . . . toothaches
> . . . childbirth . . . curtains . . . dishtowels . . . kerosene oil . . . lamp chimneys . . . coal
> for the stove . . . diapers . . . mittens . . . soap and hunger? . . . And all of a sudden
> . . . she'd jump up, smack her hands together and say, "Atcha dratcha!" . . . and she'd
> come back revived and refreshed and ready to go at them drat troubles. (2)

Marge bursts into tears at the end of Mildred's story, and Mildred tells her that
the rest of the crowd had a similar reaction upon recognizing their own grand-
mothers in Mildred's story. In describing her grandmother's daily battle for her
family's survival, Mildred both validates black women's contributions and educates readers about the specific struggles that black women face.

Throughout her columns, Childress shows Mildred refuting the stereotypical view of black domestics as passive and happy to serve their white employers.
However, she refuses to make Mildred try to conform to the dominant image
of femininity. To the contrary, Mildred flat out rejects the domestic ideology of
the age, showing the ways that this ideology excludes black women.[13] In "All the
Things We Are," Childress critiques "the ideal American woman," pointing out
the time and money it would take to be able to fit this ideal (*Like* 67). She goes
through a list of the things she would need to have to look the part: perfume, fals-
ies, a manicure, a pedicure, a new hairstyle, a girdle, a variety of creams, makeup,
hair curlers and straighteners, clothing for every occasion, and a variety of under-
clothes. And in order to act the part, she would need several hours of leisure time:

> I should have one hour a day just to loll aroun' in my scented tub while I think
> pretty thoughts. I need time to shop carefully and make sure that I'm buyin' only
> the things that suit my very own personality. I need time to plan well-balanced
> meals, I need time to go to the drug store and buy vitamins and all them toiletries.
> I need time to purchase newspapers and more magazines. I need time to do some
> volunteer work for churches and clubs, and I need time to answer all mail promptly
> and keep up with invitations and entertain lightly after the theatre. (66–67)

In making her readers aware of the impossibility for a working-class woman to
be able to afford both the time and money to achieve such an ideal, she eluci-
dates class differences among women. As she shows in other columns, her labor

and the labor of other black women make this leisure time possible for the white, middle-class women who represent the domestic ideal.

Other columns address the political repression of the McCarthy era, helping readers understand the hypocrisy of the anticommunist crusade. In one column, Mildred complains to Marge, "Every word you read is Communist this and Communist that and McCarthy, McCarthy, McCarthyism." She goes on to protest the investigations of Communist influence in churches, schools, libraries, the military, clubs, businesses, and political organizations, as well as the harassment of factory workers, writers, artists, and everyday citizens. "And for what?" she asks Marge. "WHY?" In the remainder of the column, she helps Marge to see that McCarthyism thwarts the very freedoms it claims to protect. She argues that anticommunism detracts energy from the pursuit of justice, indicating that justice involves addressing such issues as health care, housing, and equal resources for schools and communities. "The question today is *not* McCarthyism or Communism," she informs Marge. "It is—American Justice." She closes the column by telling Marge, "There are two doors in front of us: Persecution or Justice, and it's up to the American People to decide which one it will be. . . . I've made up my mind, Marge, How about you" ("Conversation" 4). In ending with this question, she encourages readers to respond to the question themselves and invites them to join her in her quest for justice. As in her other works, she encourages women's activism, yet she shows an awareness of readers' fears.

Several other columns take into account readers' fears of punishment if they take a stand for justice. In "Where Is the Speakin' Place?" Mildred questions how anyone could remain silent in the face of racial violence. She tells Marge:

> It would torment my very soul if I had to shut up and pretend like they never murdered a little boy in Mississippi 'cause he was colored. I couldn't sleep at night thinkin' about all those ministers that was arrested 'cause they wanted the same kinda rights that I had! I couldn't sleep 'cause I'd be sick and 'shamed-to-my-heart that I dared not mention a word about it. (*Like* 194–95)

While Mildred unhesitatingly supports speaking out against such incidents, Childress uses Marge to anticipate her readers' fears of possible consequences. Mildred responds to Marge's unrecorded comment:

> Yes, I guess you got a point there! Of course, some people might not like them speakin' up. But the people who wouldn't like it would be the ones who either wanted to murder folks or else wanted to see *somebody else* keep on doin' it. And I wouldn't care whether folks like that liked it or not! . . . As short as life is, I sure wouldn't want to go to my grave havin' missed a chance to put in a little comment about this old world! (196)

By pointing out that people in power benefit from maintaining status quo, while the oppressed continue to suffer the consequences, Mildred emphasizes that people have a responsibility to speak out against injustice. She is critical of an age in which people are condemned for fighting against injustice and on the side of decency.

In another column, Mildred describes an interaction with some employers when she tries to sell them tickets to a Paul Robeson tribute. They warn her against getting involved with Robeson because he "is the kind of man who gets people into trouble. You don't want to get in trouble, do you?" they ask Mildred ("Old" 8).[14] Mildred responds by describing the injustices that blacks have faced throughout US history, from slavery to segregated schools and hospitals, to Jim Crow laws, to lynching. She ends the story by describing how Robeson has fought tirelessly for justice while whites have continually made false promises about equality. When she finishes relating the incident to Marge, she tells her, "Somebody has made trouble for me but it ain't Paul Robeson. And the more he speaks the less trouble I'll have. . . . [T]he last thing he will ever do is to make trouble—for me! Does peace and friendship and equality and freedom spell trouble to you?" (8). Through her defense of Robeson, Mildred tries to help readers understand the necessity of activism, despite propaganda that discourages them from standing up for their rights. She uses Robeson's persecution as an example of the ways that anticommunism works to silence people who are working on her readers' behalf.

In "Discontent," she educates her readers about the gains won by protest movements. In this story, Mildred comes across a street speaker who is protesting against segregation, unemployment, and the high cost of living. A woman in the crowd complains, "If he don't like it here, why don't he go somewhere else!" (*Like* 175). Mildred confronts the woman, following her down the street as she starts to walk away. "Listen here, lady," she tells her. "You work eight hours a day instead of twelve or fourteen because a gang of dissatisfied folks raised sand until they made it a law, and if they had all gone somewhere else you would still be on the job now instead of on your way home for supper" (175). She goes on to describe all the other gains made by the labor movement: ending child labor and establishing a minimum wage, Social Security, and unemployment insurance. She also lists gains made by other protest movements, such as women's suffrage, housing projects, and public education. In reminding her readers of these accomplishments, she defines protest as an American act, freeing it (at least in her readers' minds) from the un-American stigma of the McCarthy era.

Other columns emphasize the value of interracial coalitions. In "Somehow I'd Like to Thank Them," Mildred honors the antiracist work done by whites. She tells Marge, "It takes a lot of strength for a white person who has privilege to take a just stand for everybody's right. . . . And I feel as proud of them as I do of my folks who are fightin' to go to school and get all of *their* rights. There are a lot of good folks on this earth!" (*Like* 218–19). On another occasion, Mildred tells Marge about meeting a white domestic worker in the laundry room. When the woman snubs her, Mildred wants to haul off and "pop her in the mouth" (107), but instead she points out to the woman that, by nature of their work, they are both exploited by their employers. She then tells her, "I am not your enemy, so don't get mad with me just because you ain't free! . . . How come you can't see that it's a whole lot safer and makes more sense to put your hand in mine and be friends?" (108–09). The story ends with the woman wanting to be friends, and Mildred tells Marge, "I was so glad I hadn't popped her" (109). She recognizes that she should try to make alliances along class lines, acknowledging the need for interracial working-class solidarity.

Mildred's vision of a better world also incorporates an international perspective. Several columns link antiracist struggle in the United States to struggles against colonialism in Africa and the West Indies. In an issue of *Freedom* that focuses on Africa, Childress educates readers about connections between the struggles against racial oppression in South Africa and in the United States, letting them know why Africa's struggle is relevant to their own. She describes "an African meetin'" to Marge:

> Another speaker told us about history and slavery and all such as that, finally ending up with today and what's going on *now*. And believe me when I say THINGS ARE POPPIN'! . . . It seems that the South Africans are breakin' the Jim Crow laws! . . . Just like if you was to walk in a Mississippi waitin' room, tear down the "white" sign and sit yourself down! (*Like* 100)

In another column, Mildred helps organize a club that will work with "organizations that was tryin' to make things better for everybody." Mildred makes sure that the club will feature speakers to educate club members "about African and West Indian people." When she tells Marge about the club, she says, "Girl, it makes me feel good all over to know that from now on in, my good times will count for somethin' that'll help people and make the world a better place to live in" (*Like* 75). Her concern extends beyond improving her own situation or fighting for justice in the United States; her goal is to work to end oppression in an international context.

In "If Heaven Is What We Want," Mildred describes her vision of the ideal society she wants to create:

> I want to go to the section of Heaven that's all mixed with different kinds of folks. . . . I want to have a nice little house on a block that's peopled by all the kinds of people there are. And I want us all to get to know each other real well and learn to speak at least one common language so that we can talk to each other about everything there is! . . . I want to meet ship-buildin' people, dancin' people, lawyers

and doctors and vacuum cleaner salesmen, and subway motormen and poets and newspaper people and folks who pick fruit and plant fields and some of all the kind of folks. . . . I'd like you to leave out the bombs and wars. You can keep all the dispossess and charity agencies, also the miseries and diseases, the hatreds, the floods and tornadoes, Jim Crow houses and schools, and all manner of ugly things like that. (*Like* 192–93)

She envisions a peaceful gathering of races, classes, and workers, one in which all people value and respect each other and no one group of people benefits at the expense of another.

The vision she describes is similar to one that Lloyd L. Brown uses to close *Iron City*, his 1951 prison novel of three black Communist organizers (in jail for their Communist activities) who fight to save the life of a young black man wrongly charged with murder. Brown's novel ends with the dream sequence of Henry Faulcon, one of the organizers. Faulcon's dream involves a mass meeting that displaces those with wealth and power and encourages equality and unity between races, genders, and classes. In his foreword to the 1994 edition of *Iron City*, Alan Wald writes that Faulcon's dream "constitutes a powerful affirmation of socialism—not as an externally imposed abstraction, but as the concrete expression of the aspirations of a people. Socialism's universalizing tendencies are depicted as growing out of national culture and experience" (xxvii). Like Faulcon's dream, Mildred's vision (in this passage and throughout all her columns) is drawn from her own experiences and is grounded in a profound belief in change and her desire to create a more just and decent world.

Childress and Brown were good friends, and the parallels between their two dream sequences are hardly coincidental. Even though Brown's novel focuses on the male prisoners, he honors the crucial role that women play in the prisoners' struggle. Childress puts a black woman at the center of the struggle, but their dreams remain the same. Childress does more than just replace Brown's Communist male heroes with a woman, though. She brings black women's issues to the forefront and incorporates them into the struggle to create a more just and equitable society. Through Mildred, Childress helped her black, working-class, female readers envision ways that they could participate in building a better world. Childress's writings from this period not only laid the groundwork for a dialogue about black women's issues within the Left, but also provided models of resistance for black women to become involved.

In many of her later essays and interviews, Childress discusses how she strove to be a writer who challenged stereotypical representations of black women. In "A Candle in a Gale Wind," she writes that she tried to portray "those seldom singled out by the mass media, except as source material for derogatory humor and/or condescending clinical, social analysis" (*Like* 112). Childress downplayed her Left past, as do most of her critics, who point to her representations of strong black female characters as precursors to black feminist thought. Yet the feminist dynamic of Childress's work cannot be fully understood without re-course to her roots in the Left. Re-situating Childress within her proper place in Left cultural history can help show a continuous tradition of black feminist thought that did not just emerge new in the 1960s and 1970s but was growing and evolving in earlier decades.

CHAPTER 4

Antiracism, Anticolonialism, and the Contradictory Left Feminism of Lorraine Hansberry

We are savage in our contradictions, we humans, Ah savage!
—Lorraine Hansberry, letter to a friend

When Lorraine Hansberry arrived in New York City in 1950, she moved into the same building as Claudia Jones and quickly became involved with a cadre of black women activists who were helping redefine the Left's approach to the Woman Question in order to address the specific problems facing black women. These women included Jones; Thelma Dale, a leader in the Harlem Left and a founding member of the Congress of American Women; and Alice Childress, a militant playwright who helped start the Communist-led Sojourners for Truth and Justice. The various women in this Left feminist community emphasized the centrality of black women's leadership in antiracist and labor movements and addressed such issues as workplace discrimination, the need to unionize domestic workers, and the importance of interracial unity. In the cultural realm, they argued for the need to present images of militant black women as alternatives to the stereotypical representations of black women in film and television shows.

Hansberry incorporated this Left feminist perspective in the articles that she wrote for *Freedom* and the lesbian journal *The Ladder*, as well as in many of her nonfiction writings and speeches. Her rather hefty FBI file, her history of activism, and her journalism illustrate the story of a woman unafraid to speak her mind, despite the consequences of McCarthyism. In her public persona, she never backed down from her Left stance. At first glance, though, her plays do not seem to reflect the Left feminist ideas she wrote about in her journal articles. But a careful reading of her dramatic works reveals the strategic ways in which she constructed representations of women who controlled the destiny of the play, thus emphasizing the key roles that black women have historically played in struggles against racism and colonialism.

Hansberry's plays challenged the dominant domestic ideology of the age by focusing on black women's roles in antiracist and anticolonial struggles and emphasizing black women's strength. While her female characters do not take on leadership roles or fight for their own liberation as women, they still play important roles in struggles against both racism and colonialism by fostering men's political development and helping them to tap into a tradition of black resistance. The three female characters in *A Raisin in the Sun* present inspirational alternatives to the dominant image of femininity. Mama fights for her family's survival and struggles to teach her children the value of freedom and dignity. Beneatha challenges feminine standards through her decision to wear her hair "natural" and through her pursuit of a career rather than a husband. And although Ruth values her family, she considers an abortion because she and Walter cannot provide for another child. Other Hansberry plays feature similarly powerful black women: in *The Drinking Gourd*, a slave mother who arms her children and sends them off to freedom, and in *Les Blancs*, a black woman warrior who spurs a reluctant African man to join the armed insurgency against colonial rule. In an era in which the prevailing domestic ideology excluded black and working-class women, Hansberry deserves credit for creating characters who challenged the dominant images of femininity.

Earlier drafts of *A Raisin in the Sun* and *Les Blancs* suggest that she had originally intended to have women as the main characters.[1] But in later drafts, she makes men the central characters in these plays, while the women take on supporting roles. Looking at these two plays, as well as *The Drinking Gourd* (her one dramatic work with a central female character), in the context of these revisions, as well as Hansberry's Left feminist journal articles, can help locate the Left feminist undertones in Hansberry's plays. Although most of her plays do not overtly reflect her ties to a Left feminist community, the silences and tensions in these plays can tell us something about the difficulties in writing from a Left feminist perspective, even with a strong community of support.

Part of the difficulty in locating a Left feminist voice in many of Hansberry's plays is that her Left feminist community was not her sole community of support. She had connections to the Communist Party in Chicago, Madison, and Harlem, as well as to black nationalist groups. She worked at *Freedom* and had close relationships to Jones, Dale, Childress, and other militant black feminists. She also had important ties to the theater world and the bohemian enclave in Greenwich Village. Until shortly before her death at the age of thirty-four, she was married to Robert Nemiroff, a white, Jewish Communist. But while married to Nemiroff, she was also part of a predominantly white circle of lesbians, most of whom did not share her Left politics. And although she was committed to the struggles of the working class, she came from a privileged economic background. These various and often-conflicting allegiances can, to a certain extent, account for the split between her nonfiction writings and her plays. But looking at the conflicts and contradictions in her work can provide a deeper understanding not only of the complexity of her political philosophy but also of some of the difficulties and challenges for black women on the Left during this time.

In "The Problem with Lorraine Hansberry" (1979), the poet and feminist critic Adrienne Rich discusses her frustration with the discontinuity between the radical black feminist voice in many of Hansberry's nonfiction writings and the lack of it in her plays. She wonders about Hansberry's feminist influences and identifies Hansberry's "problem" as her isolation within a predominantly white, male community (252–53). Likewise, in *Women in Theatre: Compassion and Hope*, feminist drama critic Karen Malpede criticizes Hansberry for retreating from female-centered dramas and wonders if Hansberry lacked a feminist community. Malpede asks, "Did [Hansberry] censor herself, knowing she would be censored? Or did the forms of a woman-centered drama still elude her because the feminist community was not yet strong enough to provide the actual examples required?"(164). But Hansberry's connection to Jones and the other women in her Left feminist community suggests that, far from struggling to survive within the Left as a lone voice of feminist critique, Hansberry had multiple sources of support. While Rich and Malpede suggest that Hansberry suppressed her radical feminism for fear of censorship by males within her community, her involvement with this Left feminist community tells a different story.[2] I turn briefly to examine her process of political development, to establish her solid entrenchment in a community of women on the Left who were instrumental in challenging stereotypical and degrading images of black women and foregrounding the central leadership roles that black women have played in freedom struggles, both in the United States and internationally.

In her remarks at a 1964 memorial service for W.E.B. Du Bois, the militant black leader who had spent his lifetime challenging racial and colonial oppression, Hansberry encouraged black Americans to follow Du Bois's example, to "look toward and work for a socialist organization of society" ("Legacy" 20). As Paul Robeson noted in disappointment, Hansberry was the only participant in a room full of radicals to mention the Communist Party (in Duberman 524). In this speech, one of Hansberry's last public appearances before her untimely death from cancer at the age of thirty-four, Hansberry states that she never found any "cause to detour from these great notions of the master"; and, indeed, she remained faithful to a socialist vision throughout her brief lifetime ("Legacy" 20). Having witnessed the mob violence at Robeson's Peekskill concert, Claudia Jones's arrest and deportation for Smith Act violations, and the persecution of Robeson, Du Bois, and countless other friends and acquaintances for their Communist Party ties, she was well aware of the damaging effects of the anticommunist crusade. But in her public persona, she never backed down from her Left stance. From her 1949 letter to the judge of Foley Square in New York, protesting the trial of Jones and ten other Party leaders who had been arrested under the Smith Act, to her 1962 speech at a mass meeting to abolish the House Un-American Activities Committee (HUAC), she was uncompromising in her critique of McCarthyism and her commitment to her radical politics.

Hansberry's FBI file consists of three thick binders that trace her involvement with pro-Communist organizations going back to the age of eighteen, when she was a student at the University of Wisconsin.[3] Hansberry biographer Margaret Wilkerson's research suggests that Hansberry's Party associations go back even farther; she mentions a close acquaintance of the Hansberry family who was largely responsible for her political education. This man, a local Party official, had lived in the apartment below the Hansberrys' when Lorraine was ten or eleven. According to Wilkerson, he "provided the framework" for her radical politics ("Excavating" 78–79). In addition to her lengthy conversations with this mentor, she met a number of prominent black activists through her parents, who were active leaders within the black community on Chicago's South Side. Family friends included Robeson, Du Bois, and Langston Hughes. Her uncle William Leo Hansberry, a professor of African history and culture at Howard University, frequently brought African students with him to visit, encouraging her early interest in colonial struggles and black nationalism. Growing up in the midst of a politically conscious household, Hansberry learned the value of socialism and black militancy at a young age.

Soon after arriving at the University of Wisconsin in 1948, she became involved with various Communist Party causes: she joined (and later became chair of) the Young Progressives of America (a Communist-led organization), attended Party meetings, and worked briefly on Henry Wallace's Progressive Party campaign (a campaign heavily supported by the Communist Party). Most likely, Hansberry had little opportunity to discuss women's issues or oppression within these organizations; some of her later writings indicate her frustration with the sexist attitudes of the men involved in these organizations during her brief college career. In "All the Dark and Beautiful Warriors," an unpublished and partly autobiographical novel manuscript, Hansberry tells the story of Candace, a young black woman who insists that revolutionary politics must take sexual politics into account. Like Hansberry, Candace comes from a wealthy family on the South Side of Chicago and attends the University of Wisconsin. During Candace's years as a student, she becomes romantically involved with Monasse, an African student. In a conversation regarding one of Candace's friends who has become pregnant out of wedlock, Monasse insinuates that she is "a little free" and that her behavior is altogether unacceptable for "a decent young woman." When Candace questions him about the man's behavior, he claims, "One only presumes in the first place with certain kinds of girls." Candace calls him on his sexual double standard, but he tells her he has no "intention of discussing this matter with a young woman I respect." She fires back, "And you call yourself a revolutionary!" His inability to link gender emancipation to racial or national freedom frustrates her, and she vows to herself that "on behalf of American women—and world emancipation—she would change his mind about a number of things" (in *To Be Young* 83–85).

Deciding "to pursue an education of another kind" (*To Be Young* 93), she left school after a year and a half and, in 1950, moved to New York City, where she found greater support for women's issues within the radical community of the Harlem Left. Within a few months of arriving in New York, she began working at *Freedom*, Robeson's militant black newspaper. In the *Freedom* office, Hansberry found a strong commitment to black women's issues. Editor Louis Burnham allowed her free reign to integrate a feminist analysis with the paper's international socialist point of view,[4] and she worked with several women whose writing and activism helped foster her Left feminist politics, including general manager Thelma Dale, labor reporter Yvonne Gregory, and Alice Childress.

In addition to the Left feminist community at *Freedom*, she had a close relationship with Claudia Jones.[5] A year before Hansberry's arrival in New York, *Political Affairs* had published Jones's "An End to the Neglect of the Problems of the Negro Woman!" Jones's influence on Hansberry can be seen clearly in Hansberry's *Freedom* articles, many of which draw on issues raised in Jones's article. Hansberry's first article for *Freedom*, which appeared in the June 1951 issue, critiqued the "distorted and degraded image of the American Negro" on television and radio and clearly drew on Jones's critique of cultural stereotypes of black women ("Negroes" 7). Jones argued that black women are misrepresented in the cultural realm, where the black woman "is the victim of the white chauvinist stereotype as to where her place should be. In the film, radio, and press, the Negro woman is not pictured in her real role as breadwinner, mother, and protector of the family" ("End" 55). Instead, Jones argued, the culture industry portrayed black women as subservient to their white employers and as always putting "the care of children and families of others above her own" ("End" 55). Likewise, Hansberry criticized *The Beulah Show* for its portrayal of "a giggling, contented domestic, who, according to the producer and writers lives only to take care of her white employers and their children" ("Negroes" 7). Several months later, Childress took up the issue of black domestic workers in her Mildred columns, which appeared as a regular *Freedom* feature beginning in October 1951. And Dale had been organizing for domestic worker rights and criticizing Hollywood's representations of blacks in movies in her work with the National Negro Congress and the Congress of American Women (CAW).

Hansberry was also involved with the Sojourners for Truth and Justice, an organization founded to coordinate black women's political activities and fight for black liberation. The leadership was made up almost entirely of pro-Communist women, including Jones and Childress. In her *Freedom* coverage of the October 1951 Sojourners for Truth and Justice rally in Washington, D.C., Hansberry provided specific examples of women's courage and determination, giving story after story of women whose husbands or children had been victims of racial violence. These experiences, rather than silencing or frightening these women, served to make them militant activists, united in their efforts to bring about justice (Hansberry, "Women"). Her coverage of the rally helped show why black women should be given more leadership roles within the Left. Like her piece on the Sojourners for Truth rally, many of Hansberry's *Freedom* articles document black women's activism and leadership. These articles support Jones's assertion that "Negro women have become symbols of many present-day struggles of the Negro people" because they "are the real active forces—the organizers and workers in all the institutions and organizations of the Negro people" ("End" 51, 57).

While working at *Freedom*, Hansberry was also studying black nationalism with Du Bois at the Jefferson School. The Council on African Affairs, run by Du Bois and Robeson, was in the same building as the *Freedom* office. Many of her *Freedom* articles incorporate her burgeoning interest in colonial struggles in Africa and Latin America. Both she and Childress shared an interest in women's participation in international revolutionary movements. Childress's musical revue *Gold through the Trees* emphasized women's contributions to black liberation struggles throughout the world and at different moments in history. In her review of *Gold* for *Freedom*, Hansberry raved about the representations of an African queen watching her husband being taken away in chains, of Harriet Tubman leading former slaves to freedom, of a Haitian woman aiding Toussaint Louverture in the Haitian slave revolt, and of a Martinsville woman whose son has been lynched. Hansberry described Childress's revue as "probably the most worthwhile and entertaining show currently running in New York" ("CNA").

Like Childress's musical revue, many of Hansberry's *Freedom* articles emphasize women's participation in international struggles against colonialism. In her article on Egypt's demand for independence from Britain, she focuses on the Daughters of the Nile, a women's movement that trained young women in guerilla warfare and demanded for women the right to vote and hold public office. The article features one young Egyptian woman, describing her as symbolizing "the Egyptian people's part in the spirit of the liberation that is sweeping all of Africa" ("Egyptian" 3). Her article on the 1952 Inter-Continental Peace Congress in Montevideo, Uruguay, also addresses the important role that women play in revolutionary movements. This conference, organized by the American Peace Crusade and the New York Peace Institute, had been banned in both Chile and Argentina due to pressure from the US State Department. It was held in Montevideo despite the government's opposition. Hansberry attended as a substitute for Paul Robeson, whose passport had been revoked by the State Department; her own passport was revoked when she returned. In her article for *Freedom*, Hansberry praises women's courage and determination in the struggle to promote peace and justice and links their struggle to that of women in the United States ("Illegal"). In a speech given shortly after her return, Hansberry discusses her participation in the women's meeting, where she was chosen as one of three women to sit at the front of the room. In this speech, Hansberry mentions having to pretend one meeting was a social event when a police officer unexpectedly entered the room ("Report").

In 1953, Hansberry married Robert Nemiroff, a white, Jewish Communist, whom she had met a few years earlier on a picket line, protesting a whites-only basketball team at New York University. In Nemiroff, she found a partner who shared her radical convictions; fittingly, they attended a protest against Ethel and Julius Rosenberg's execution the day before their wedding. After marrying Nemiroff, she stopped working fulltime at *Freedom* so that she could concentrate more fully on her creative work. For the next few years, she wrote occasional pieces for *Freedom* and other publications while working on and off for Rachel Productions and the People's Artists, Incorporated, two artistic agencies run by Communist Party supporters. While she devoted most of her energy to playwriting, she worked at various odd jobs until 1956, when one of Nemiroff's songs became a hit, giving her the financial security to stop working and focus on her plays.

As she worked on her first play, Hansberry continued to write articles that reflected her Left feminist politics, often refining and expanding the ideas debated in the Party presses in the late 1940s and early 1950s. She begins "In Defense of the Equality of Men" with a critique of *Modern Woman: The Lost Sex*, a book that equated women's independence, intellectual pursuits, and careers with being "lost" and urged women to return to the home and embrace domesticity in order to reclaim their femininity. Jones, Elizabeth Gurley Flynn, and other Party women had lambasted the book when it originally appeared in 1947, comparing it to the fascist ideology of Adolph Hitler's Germany. Hansberry similarly attacks the current domestic ideology, critiquing the idea of what she refers to as "charts" for acceptable masculine and feminine behavior ("In Defense" 2066).[6]

While articles in the *Worker*, *Masses and Mainstream*, and *Political Affairs* critiqued the exclusion of black and working-class women from the dominant images of femininity, Hansberry extended this analysis to sexuality. As a practicing yet closeted lesbian, she noticed similarities between homosexual oppression and the oppression suffered by blacks and women. Unfortunately, she lacked a forum for discussing the political dimensions of her sexuality. Within the Communist Party, discussion of homosexuality was considered taboo, and her lesbian community did not share her political passions. In "The Double Life of Lorraine Hansberry" (1999), Elise Harris claims that Hansberry suffered further alienation as the only black woman in her lesbian circle; Hansberry often turned to James Baldwin (also black and gay) to help her cope with the whiteness of her lesbian crowd, but he did not share her concern with gender oppression (100). Not surprisingly, she rarely wrote on the issue of homosexuality; her only published work on the issue can be found in her two anonymous letters to the lesbian publication, *The Ladder*, signed simply "L.H.N." or "L. N."[7] In one of these letters, she argues that women who wanted to challenge the domestic ideology needed to take sexuality into account, as "homosexual persecution and condemnation has at its roots not only social ignorance, but a philosophically active anti-feminist dogma" (L. N. 30). In her other *Ladder* letter, she compares the pressure on both blacks and homosexuals to conform to the dominant culture, arguing that both groups are stigmatized by their inability to fit the mainstream norms (L.H.N. 26–28).

While none of her plays have a lesbian character, Hansberry strove to challenge the dominant domestic ideology by creating female characters who were not white, middle-class, married homemakers. Hansberry originally planned to call her first play "The Crystal Stair," a title borrowed from the Langston Hughes poem, "Mother to Son."[8] Hughes's poem recounts the struggles of a working-class black woman who tells her son, "Life for me ain't been no crystal stair. . . . But all the time / I'se been a-climbin' on (187). Hansberry's original title suggests that she intended to make this mother's struggle the focus of the play. However, she eventually renamed it *A Raisin in the Sun* (a line also taken from a Hughes poem), a play that has several strong female characters but centers on Walter Lee Younger's journey into manhood.

A Raisin in the Sun focuses on Walter's struggle between his individual desire for material wealth and the collective good of the family and the black race. However, his struggle does not take place in isolation. Walter has a community of women who give him strength, who push him to think about the family and the race, rather than just himself. At the beginning of the play, Walter's frustration and resentment dominate every scene. Rather than turning to Mama, his wife, Ruth, or his sister, Beneatha, for support, he blames them for his failures. As he tells Ruth, "That is just what is wrong with the colored woman in this world. . . . Don't understand about building their men up and making 'em feel like they somebody. Like they can do something. . . . We one group of men tied to a race of women with small minds" (34–35). Later, he yells at Mama, "You butchered up a dream of mine—you—who always talking 'bout your children's dreams" (95). Rather than looking at the societal factors that contribute to his position in life, he blames his problems on his wife and mother, viewing them as impediments to his progress. By the end of the play, however, he begins to identify white supremacy as the source of his oppression and lack of opportunities for economic advancement. When "he finally come into his manhood" (151), as Mama describes his process of learning to resist white power, it is because he draws on the voices of Mama, Ruth, and Beneatha.

Hansberry presents Mama as the cultivator and the nurturer of her family; she passes on the spirit of empowerment and resistance to her children. While Walter thinks mostly of himself, her concern is always with the collective family good. Her choice to use the insurance money from Big Walter's death to buy a house in the all-white Clybourne Park neighborhood is not about the desire to assimilate into white society; she wants to move her family to a safer neighborhood. She tries to teach her children that freedom and dignity are worth fighting for. When Walter wants to accept an offer by a white neighborhood association to keep the family out of the neighborhood, she tells him, "Son—I come from five generations of people who was slaves and sharecroppers—but ain't nobody in my family never let nobody pay 'em no money that was a way of telling us we wasn't fit to walk the earth. We ain't never been that poor" (143). Walter, however, disregards the lessons she has taught him, agreeing to the offer after squandering the insurance money on a risky liquor store venture.

Like Mama, Ruth's actions are guided by the desire for a better life for her family. When she unexpectedly becomes pregnant, she considers having an abortion, knowing that she would not be able to provide a new child with a safe and secure life and that a new child would take away resources from her child that is already living. However, once Mama puts a down payment on the new house, Ruth decides to keep the baby, knowing she will have a healthier and more secure environment in which to raise the new baby. Walter's dream, on the other hand, centers on his own self-enhancement and providing his family with wealth and material goods. He wants to use the insurance money to invest in a liquor store, a venture he is convinced will bring huge profits. While Walter dreams of a future filled with flashy cars and pearls, Ruth directs her energy toward creating a stable life for her family in the present. When Walter loses the insurance money and Mama decides not to move, Ruth tries to convince her that they must do whatever is necessary to hold onto the vision of a better life that the house represents. "I'll work twenty hours a day in all the kitchens in Chicago. . . . I'll strap my baby on my back if I have to and scrub all the floors in America and wash all the sheets in America if I have to—but we got to MOVE! We got to get OUT OF HERE!" (140).

While Mama and Ruth devote themselves to preserving their families, Beneatha thinks about advancing the race. Unlike Walter, she does not disregard Mama's lessons. From her lecture to George on why she hates "assimilationist Negroes" (81) to her sarcastic remarks about a neighbor who quotes Booker T. Washington, her voice of protest against white supremacy remains constant throughout the play. She embraces her African heritage, even though her obsession with African culture and history amuse her family and irritate her brother. He is unable to appreciate the need to fight collectively against racist ideology until the end of the play.

In the play's final scene, Walter has called Karl Lindner to tell him that he has decided to accept his offer. Mama feels Walter has failed to live up to her expectations for him, yet she refuses to give up on him. Although Ruth wants to send Travis out of the room, Mama makes him stay to hear Walter accept Lindner's offer. "You make him understand what you doing, Walter Lee. You teach him good," she tells him. "You show where our five generations done come to" (147). When Walter is faced with the responsibility of teaching his own son a lesson, he finally grasps the significance of the words Mama, Ruth, and Beneatha have been uttering throughout the play. He refuses Lindner's offer in a speech that relates the family's strength and perseverance and claims a sense of pride and dignity for their struggle. In the end, Walter changes from wanting to acquire material goods to wanting to provide his son with a more just and dignified life, as Mama and Ruth have been struggling to do throughout the play. And from Beneatha, he has learned the necessity of fighting collectively against white power.

Several critics have viewed Walter's final act as revolutionary, including Julius Lester, who compares Walter's refusal to take Lindner's money to Rosa Parks's refusal to give up her seat on the bus. Lester claims, "In that quiet dissent, both of them said Yes to human dignity. They said No to those who would define them and thereby deny their existence, and by saying No, they began to define themselves" (267). Hansberry, however, noted that she intended Mama to be the Rosa Parks figure. In an unpublished essay, she writes, "It is she who . . . scrubs the floors of a nation in order to create black diplomats and university professors. It is she, while seeming to cling to traditional restraints, who drives the young on into the fire hoses. And one day simply refuses to move to the back of the bus in Montgomery" (Nemiroff, *Lorraine* 158). But Hansberry makes Walter's voice the dominant one at the end of the play, even though Walter would not become the strong and committed man who understands his family's historical legacy of struggle and resistance without the words and lessons of Mama, Ruth, and Beneatha.

In her 1960 essay, "This Complex of Womanhood," Hansberry argues that black women should be recognized for their central role in resistance movements. Her essay echoes many of the sentiments that Claudia Jones had articulated over a decade earlier in "An End to the Neglect of the Problems of the Negro Woman!" Jones's article sought to give recognition to "the militant participation of Negro women in all aspects of the struggle for peace, civil rights, and economic security"; she argued that "Negro women are the real active forces—the organizers and workers—in all the institutions and organizations of the Negro people" ("End" 51, 57). Hansberry made a similar argument about the need to recognize women's contributions and closed her essay by stating, "[On] behalf of an ailing world, which sorely needs our defiance, may we, as Negroes or *women*, never accept the notion of our place" ("This Complex" 40). Elsewhere, Hansberry asserted that radical feminists who fought for freedom and equality constituted the true "American patriot[s]" and argued that women's liberation—and women's leadership—was integral to bringing about that better world ("In Defense" 2062, 2065). And in a 1956 letter to the editor of the *Village Voice*, Hansberry wrote that art that tries to justify the concept of "'woman's place' is tiresome, foolish, and dreadfully out of keeping" with a belief in women's equality ("On Strinberg" 172).

Despite Hansberry's intentions to cast Mama as a strong black woman whose freedom and racial pride remain constant throughout the play, white audiences tended to view her as the stereotypical black mother that they were accustomed to seeing on stage and screen: the patient and stoic black mother who loves and nurtures both her own family and the white folks for whom she works. As Ossie Davis points out, in Mama, white audiences "could find somebody they could trust absolutely up there on that stage—somebody so familiar to them—so comfortable" (400). This Mama figure, popular in many movies and films of the 1940s and 1950s, was safe because she accepted her place and did not question white supremacy. She posed no threat to white America. The early drafts of both the play and the movie, though, indicate that Hansberry intended Mama to be more militant than she is in the Broadway production. The original draft of the play ends with the family living in their new house and threatened by a racist mob. In this version, Mama patrols the house with a loaded gun in order to protect the family (Carter 50).[9]

In a scene cut from the movie, Mama describes an incident in which she had asked a former employer for a raise and had been told that domestic work was not a job. The white woman for whom she works told her she was "just another part of the family" (surely a nod to Childress and her *Freedom* columns on domestic worker issues, collected in the anthology *Like One of the Family*). She quit after that incident, refusing to let a white woman determine the conditions of her employment (Hansberry, *Raisin* 40). Hansberry's decision to allow this scene to be cut is surprising because her first article for *Freedom* had critiqued cultural representations of black domestic workers. She criticized one show in particular for its portrayal of a domestic worker "who, according to the producer and writers lives only to take care of her white employers and their children" ("Negroes").

In an unpublished essay that situates *Raisin* against the backdrop of McCarthyism, Odessa Rose looks at several scenes that were cut from the original Broadway production, cuts that she says "significantly softened the play's statement" (3). Rose attributes these cuts to fears of anticommunist repercussions and the reality that white audiences would not pay to see the play if they deemed it too controversial. However, Hansberry, who had shown no fear of repercussions in her speeches and writings, allowed these cuts to be made, even though she later regretted them. When offered a movie contract by Columbia Pictures, she vowed to emphasize the racial and class dimensions so that viewers could not misinterpret her script. While she restored several important scenes missing from the Broadway production, in the end, she did little to make the movie more radical. As the *Original Unfilmed Screenplay* indicates, the more militant scenes did not make it to the final version. Spike Lee argues that, in the movie version of *Raisin*, "all the cuts had to deal with softening a too defiant black voice" (xlvi).

In all of her plays, Beneatha is perhaps the best reflection of the Left feminist ideas in Hansberry's nonfiction work. One of Hansberry's harshest indictments of sexist society appears in a letter she wrote to a friend in 1964, in which she blames unrealistic social standards of femininity for Marilyn Monroe's suicide. She writes, "The concept of 'woman' which fashioned, warped and destroyed a human being such as Marilyn Monroe IS HIDEOUSLY WRONG" ("On Arthur" 175). She acknowledges that social norms for women affect *all* women, regardless of race, class, or sexuality, by holding women to unrealistic standards. For black women, the image is based on white standards of beauty and thus impossible to achieve. Earlier scripts suggest that Hansberry intended for Beneatha to be more outspoken against this image than the Broadway production of *Raisin* would allow. In one scene cut from this production, Beneatha crops her hair and wears it "natural." Although wearing an Afro became a statement of militancy in the 1960s, at the time, very few black women wore their hair in this style. As Rose points out, "In 1959, an afro was a political statement, one that rejected integrationist politics by rejecting white standards of beauty . . . and expressing pride in . . . black culture" (7). As Beneatha announces when she enters the room, clad in Nigerian garb and with her new hairstyle, "Enough of this assimilationist junk!" (*Raisin* 76). Hansberry insisted that this scene be restored, and the movie and subsequent editions of the play contained this scene.

In several scenes, Beneatha delivers speeches that echo Hansberry's nonfiction essays. In one essay, Hansberry writes that she has "a longing that another generation of girls will not have to grow up under a certain pragmatism which insists that men do not like 'brainy' women. . . . Girls are better taught to 'reach for the stars' even in the matter of seeking or accepting a mate" ("In Defense" 2065). Throughout *Raisin*, Beneatha searches for an intellectually gratifying and equal relationship. She rejects George Murchinson as a serious suitor because he is shallow and snobbish and thinks the idea of a female doctor is "pretty funny" (50). In one scene, when she tells him, "I love to talk," he replies, "I don't like it. You're a nice-looking girl . . . all over. That's all you need, honey, forget the atmosphere. . . . I want a nice—(Groping)—simple (Thoughtfully)—sophisticated girl . . . not a poet—OK?" She stops seeing him after this exchange, describing him to her mother afterward as a "fool" (96–97). She prefers the African revolutionary Asagai, who supports her dreams and fosters her political development.

Beneatha also protests the idea of marriage as the ultimate goal for women. Her family fails to understand her desire to be a doctor, but she does not let their lack of understanding deter her. When Walter chastises her for the cost of her education to her family, she falls to her knees and exclaims, "Forgive me for ever wanting to be anything at all!" (37). Walter has no patience for her dreams. He tells her that she should "just get married and be quiet" (38). While Mama and Ruth support her dream to be a doctor, they, like Walter, assume that Beneatha will, of course, want to get married. Beneatha, on the other hand, considers her career more important than romance. If she gets married at all, it will be to someone who values her for her intellect, and someone for whom ideas (and the issue of one's place in the world) are meaningful.

Hansberry's experience as a lesbian in a heterosexual marriage perhaps influenced her critique of marriage. Elise Harris describes Hansberry's marriage to

Nemiroff as a close and affectionate friendship, based on their mutual commitment to Left politics and culture. Like most celebrities at the time, Hansberry remained closeted, maintaining what Harris refers to as "a role model version of herself for the media stage" while she kept her relationships with women a secret (97). In one of her *Ladder* letters, Hansberry argues that most women (regardless of their sexuality) fall into the "social trap" of marriage, both in order to conform to societal expectations for women and because it is their only option for economic security. She argues that economic factors keep many women tied to their marriages with men:

> I suspect that the problem of the married woman who would prefer emotional-physical relationships with other women is proportionally much higher than a similar statistic for men. . . . [T]he estate of women being what it is, how could we ever begin to guess the numbers of women who are not prepared to risk a life alien to what they have been taught all their lives to believe was their "natural" destiny—AND—their only expectation for ECONOMIC security. (L. N. 30)

As long as marriage as an institution exists, she suggests in the rest of her letter, women (regardless of their sexual orientation) will continue to be oppressed.

However, although Beneatha rejects marriage and defies feminine conventions throughout the play, Hansberry undermines her militancy. At the end of the play, when Walter delivers his speech to Lindner, Beneatha announces her decision to marry Asagai and follow him to Africa. After Walter "finally come into his manhood," Hansberry consigns Beneatha to the traditional female role she has spent the play defying (151). Additionally, Beneatha's tendency to flit from one bourgeois hobby to the next—guitar lessons, horseback riding, photography—suggest that her politics are yet another passing fad. And other scenes suggesting Beneatha's further militancy are cut. In the original screenplay for the movie version of *Raisin*, Hansberry includes a scene between Beneatha and Asagai in a campus lounge. Although Asagai engages her intellectually, he retains traditional ideas about women's place. In this scene, she criticizes the limitations of his sexual politics. Asagai tells her, "I can take women only just so seriously," and she lectures him on his backward views on women (Nemiroff, *Raisin* 51). His ability to discuss liberation and equality while treating women in a sexist manner reflected the attitude of many men in the Left at the time. In allowing this scene to be cut from the movie, Hansberry lost the opportunity to provide a critique of this attitude.

This scene is similar to the one between Candace and Monasse in "All the Dark and Beautiful Warriors" (in *To Be Young* 83–85). Given that Hansberry has acknowledged that she based Beneatha on herself, and given that Candace is partly an autobiographical character (Candace's family background is similar to Hansberry's and she attends the University of Wisconsin), we can assume that Beneatha's and Candace's politics are Hansberry's. However, she lets Walter overshadow Beneatha in *Raisin*, and she never completed her autobiographical work. But her early notes for *Les Blancs* suggest that she intended to continue Candace's story in this play. Like *Raisin*, *Les Blancs* centers on a male struggle. In this case, Tshembe, a black intellectual who has been living in Europe, must decide whether to join the violent insurgency against colonial rule. At the beginning of this play, Tshembe returns to Africa for the funeral of his father, who helped start a resistance movement against the colonial power. However, Hansberry's early notes for the play indicate that she planned to have a woman named Candace return for her mother's funeral and become a violent revolutionary (Nemiroff, *Lorraine* 31–32). But she replaced Candace with Tshembe, and the only black woman in the play has no speaking part and no name. Her character is referred to simply as "woman."

Hansberry began to work on *Les Blancs* in 1960. She did not finish this script before her death, but Nemiroff claims that "she considered *Les Blancs* to be potentially her most important play" (*Lorraine* 33).[10] In this play, Hansberry extends her analysis of black resistance movements to an anticolonial context, focusing on Tshembe's struggle to decide whether to join the revolutionary movement that his father started. Like Mama in *Raisin*, the black woman warrior figure reminds Tshembe of his connection to his culture and his responsibility to his people and his country. She urges him to act for the revolution rather than remain a passive outsider. Hansberry emphasizes this woman's significance by using her as the play's opening image. In the stage directions for the play's prologue, Hansberry has the sounds of the African bush—birds, wild animals, and drums—playing for several minutes before the curtain is raised. As the house lights go black, the music stops, the curtain lifts, and the woman appears. She pulls a spear out of the ground and raises it high in the air, and the stage fades to black. She symbolizes strength, African culture, and the need for violent struggle. Throughout the play, Tshembe encounters her at key moments in his developing commitment to the revolution. Without her, Tshembe would not join the revolution at the end of the play. And yet, he is the central figure; she never speaks.

At the end of the first act, she appears as he engages in a discussion of racism with a white American journalist. She carries the spear and begins to dance, beckoning to Tshembe to join her. He screams, "NO! I WILL NOT GO! It is not my affair anymore! . . . I don't care what happens here. . . . I am not responsible" (81). She ignores his yells and continues her dance, throwing him the spear. In the second act, she appears twice, both times after incidents that force Tshembe to re-evaluate his relationship to the revolution. In the first instance, she appears briefly after Tshembe learns of the arrest of Kumalo, a black leader working for a peaceful resolution with the colonists. A few scenes later, two hundred black people are slaughtered in a raid on a nearby village. This time, the woman appears along with two black male revolutionaries. All three wear military fatigues and carry rifles. While one of the men gives a speech arguing that they have no choice but to use violence against the oppressors, the woman remains silent. And in the play's final scene, when Tshembe finally realizes that his refusal to be a part of the revolution supports the colonial power, he takes a stand and commits himself to the revolution. Right before the curtain falls, he cries out in anguish. The woman appears in a pool of light, showing him that she has not abandoned him; she will continue to support him—and fight with him—in the struggle.

While the woman warrior figure, in her strength and support for the revolution, runs counter to the images of black women in mainstream culture, Hansberry makes her a supporting character rather than a leader in the revolution. Likewise, in *Raisin*, she allows Walter to emerge as the hero at the end of the play, while the women discuss their pride in his development as a man. The women become overshadowed by men's process of political development. Both plays contradict her own statements that black women should not accept their "place" and that social change movements should acknowledge the centrality of black women's leadership. Hansberry's original intention to make black women the central characters in both plays suggests that she herself felt conflicted between her Left feminism and her dedication to black nationalism. Of all her plays, *The Drinking Gourd* is the most representative of Hansberry's Left feminist ideas; it is the one play in which she focuses on development of political consciousness in a woman. Significantly, the one script in which she did not replace the central female character with a man is the one script that was never produced.

NBC commissioned Hansberry to write *The Drinking Gourd* in 1959 as part of a television series celebrating the centennial of the Civil War. In this script, Hansberry sought to reclaim the history of slavery at a time when most Civil War histories focused on particular battles and most cultural works depicted the tragic defeat of the South (as in *Gone with the Wind*). At a 1961 radio symposium, "The Negro Writer in America," Hansberry discusses her motivation for writing the script:

> I am so profoundly interested to realize that in these one hundred years since the Civil War very few of our countrymen have really *believed* that their Federal Union and the defeat of the slavocracy and the negation of slavery as an institution is an admirable fact of American life. So that it is now possible to get enormous books on the Civil War and to go through the back of them and not find the word "slavery," let alone "Negro." (Nemiroff, *Lorraine* 145–46)

Her script put her on the cutting edge of the emerging historical scholarship on slavery, and she puts Rissa, a slave mother who arms her children and sends them off to freedom, at the center of that history. Although one NBC official thought the script was "superb," the station deemed it too controversial, and so they paid her for it ("rather well," in her own words) and then put it in a drawer and never produced it (Nemiroff, *Lorraine* 145).

The early scenes in *The Drinking Gourd* focus on Hannibal and his desire to escape slavery. Hannibal is concerned primarily with his own exploitation and freedom and not with challenging slavery as an institution. His efforts to subvert his position as a slave involve hiding during the day to avoid working in the fields, bribing the Master's young son with banjo lessons in order to learn how to read, and planning his escape. He fantasizes about the life of his brother Isaiah, who had escaped a few years earlier, leaving behind his family, including his young son Joshua. Hannibal craves the same lifestyle he believes his brother has achieved, but he fails to see that Isaiah's escape did nothing to alter the conditions of slavery for anyone else. Sarah, the woman with whom he is romantically involved, tells him, "I can't see how his runnin' off like that did you much good. Or your mama. Almost broke her heart, that's what. And worst of all, leavin' his poor little baby" (175). While she is able to see his struggle as part of a larger one, he is concerned with his own escape.

While Hannibal dominates the early part of the play, the focus shifts to Rissa's developing awareness of the need to take a direct stance against slavery as an institution. At the beginning of the play, Rissa is concerned primarily with her family's well-being and survival. She frets over Isaiah's fate and worries about Hannibal's safety. Her goal is to mitigate slavery for her family, not to end it. She considers Hiram Sweet to be a benevolent master, and she serves him faithfully, often defending him to Hannibal. However, after Hiram falls ill, his son Everett takes over as master. When Everett learns that Hannibal can read, he orders Zeb Dudley, the white overseer, to gouge out his eyes. After this gruesome blinding takes place, Rissa realizes that slavery, even under a relatively kind master, means a lack of control over her children's well-being. When Hiram Sweet comes to her cabin to ask for her forgiveness, claiming he had nothing to do with the incident, she holds him responsible for his son's actions. The stage directions for this scene indicate, "She looks at the master with uncompromising indictment," and he leaves the cabin without absolution and without the comfort he had come to expect (214). Even when he falls to the ground and cries out for help, she ignores his pleas, letting him die while she tends to her son.

After Rissa nurses Hannibal back to health, she helps him escape from the Sweet Plantation, along with Sarah and Joshua. In the play's final scene, she steals a gun from the Sweet house and gives it to a trembling Sarah, arming them in what will surely be a battle for their freedom. She realizes that slavery makes Hannibal's security impossible. In order to protect her family, she needs to oppose the institution as a whole. Her final gesture suggests a call for revolution. Whereas in Hansberry's other plays, the men rob the women of their voices, in *The Drinking Gourd*, Hannibal does not speak in the final scenes. He is literally blind, and without the support of his mother and Sarah, he would be incapable of escape.

As *The Drinking Gourd*, with its militant heroine, and the earlier scripts for all her other plays suggest, Hansberry intended to make black women's political leadership more central. However, rather than emphasizing the leadership roles that black women were beginning to assume in the late 1940s and 1950s, women's political commitment remains secondary to the development of political consciousness in the male figures. Given that Hansberry was publicly outspoken about her Left feminist politics, her retreat from these politics in her published plays is puzzling. But at the same time, these contradictions begin to provide some insight into the challenges faced by women on the Left during the McCarthy era. Situating Hansberry's cultural work in the context of her Left feminist thought provides a framework for reading her work that illuminates the tensions between culture and activism, and between the personal and the political, with which Hansberry and many women writers on the Left struggled in their lives, their relationships, and their cultural works.

CHAPTER 5

"Ask Him If He's Tried It at Home"

Making the Personal Political

"Look who's talking! The Great White Father, and World's Champion of Women's Rights. . . . [W]hen Dr. Barnes gives you his cure all for female troubles, ask him if he's tried it at home."
—Ruth Barnes in Michael Wilson, *Salt of the Earth*

In the pages of the Party presses and in Left discussion groups, women on the Left argued that sexism and male chauvinism permeated multiple aspects of society and that the battle against what they perceived as a fascist domestic ideology must extend to their personal and romantic relationships. Communist Party leaders instructed men to examine their own sexist behaviors and how they were manifested in their personal relationships. However, Party women did not necessarily experience the effects of this the new approach in their personal relationships. Screenwriter Norma Barzman describes the struggle between theory and practice in her relationship with her husband, screenwriter Ben Barzman: "Every night I got home in plenty of time to prepare dinner. Nevertheless, Ben grumbled. He wanted the little woman at home, feelings hard for a Communist to admit, especially one who had just spent the weekend at a meeting on 'The Woman Question' where they discussed whether to pay wives a salary" (60). One woman wrote to the *Worker* that her husband "could give an excellent lecture on the necessity to emancipate women" but never lifted a finger to help her with childcare or housework (qtd. in Rosen 31). The theme of women struggling to redefine their romantic and domestic relationships appears over and over again in the works of many women writers on the Left from this era. Such literary texts explore the problems created by this gap between theory and lived reality and show women's efforts to grapple with issues such as marriage, commitment, housework, childcare, and the division of labor; many show models for more cooperative relationships.

In many ways, this literature anticipates the slogan from the second-wave women's movement: the personal is political. In *Personal Politics*, Sara Evans argues that the women's liberation movement, in part, emerged out of the realization by women active in the civil rights movement that their political activities and quest for racial justice could not be separated from their private lives; equality and justice must be present in their personal and romantic relationships as well as in the public sphere. Evans describes one of the "hallmarks" of the emerging women's liberation movement as consciousness-raising groups, where change happened "through a process of talking together, discovering common problems, and thereby understanding the need for collective action" (134, 214). While she traces consciousness-raising to the radical Students for a Democratic Society (SDS), a New Left activist group, aspects of this form of personal and political change were present in the Left feminist circles of the postwar era and are often reflected in the literature.

Beth McHenry's *Home Is the Sailor* (1948), written in conjunction with her husband, Frederick M. "Blackie" Myers, blends a critique of gender relations with a Left feminist consciousness. The novel traces sailor Billy Farrell's development as a labor organizer for the Communist-led Marine Workers Industrial Union (MWIU). Although, in many ways, the novel's tale of Depression-era sailors fighting for better working conditions and a living wage mirrors the standard proletarian novel of the 1930s, the novel is also very much a product of the early years of the Cold War. McHenry and Myers present the Red Squad raids on the MWIU hall as threats to American democracy and the first step toward fascism, while they depict Communists as honorable Americans devoted to the best interests of both class and country. Although the novel primarily focuses on male labor struggles, its treatment of gender relationships merits attention. McHenry, who wrote about women's issues for *New Masses* and the *Daily Worker* in the 1930s, clearly influenced the representation of women in the text. Although women by no means occupy a central role in the novel, Billy's changing attitude toward women reflects the influence of women like McHenry on their male partners.

At the beginning of the novel, Billy sees women as either potential dates or prostitutes;[1] he does not view them as intellectual equals or political partners. As his political thought develops, though, he begins to view his relationships with women differently, largely due to his relationship with Vivian Hall, a social worker whose previous marriage had broken up because her husband disapproved of her political activities. When Vivian pays for her own movie ticket on their first date, Billy tells her, "Two years ago I'd have walked away from a dame who tried to pay her own way. Now it seems natural" (137). She and Billy become friends, often talking late into the night about socialism and the Soviet Union. Through Vivian, Billy meets Communists and trade unionists involved in struggles other than the MWIU, and Billy acknowledges that his friendship with Vivian "did a lot to help him understand his own role in the struggle" (138). For the first time, he begins to see women as intellectual and political equals, rather than as romantic conquests.

Yet despite his friendship with Vivian, Billy's newfound awareness of women's equality takes awhile to trickle down to his romantic relationships. Although he adores Mary O'Connell, a ship waitress whom he later marries, she still comes second to his union organizing. When Billy returns from a long trip at sea, he heads immediately for the union hall rather than calling Mary. When he finally gets around to calling her, he wonders why he did not think to call her first. "I guess it's because one thing is struggle and the other is personal," he decides (185), clearly seeing the political and the personal as two separate realms. He learns that the two realms are not as distinct as he thought, however, when he becomes seriously ill and is unable to work for a long time. During his illness, he depends on Mary for both care and financial support. When he expresses uneasiness at living on her savings, she scolds him, "When do men stop being superior beings? I used to think you were kind of smart, but you still haven't learned one little thing. That is, that when people are teamed up everything they have is theirs together" (246). Through having to depend on Mary, he learns that the collective values he emphasizes in his political battles must extend to his marriage and other personal relationships.

Home is the Sailor reflects the Left's critique of the "fascist triple K" as well as the desire on the part of many women writers on the Left to present alternatives to what they considered to be a fascist domestic ideology. Sanora Babb's *The Lost Traveler* (1958) does likewise. Babb wrote for several small Left literary magazines in the Midwest during the Great Depression; during this time, she also reported on strikes and labor theater for *New Masses* and the *Worker* (Wixon x). In 1935 she traveled with Tillie Olsen to New York to attend the American Writers Congress, and a year later she went to the Soviet Union with a group of Left-wing writers. In the late 1930s, she worked on behalf of the Spanish Republic and the Anti-Nazi League in California, where she was actively involved in a circle of Left writers and filmmakers (Wald, Introduction xi). During the 1950s, she lived in Mexico within a circle of blacklisted filmmakers in order to protect her husband, the cinematographer James Wong Howe, from blacklist by association. Many of the writers and filmmakers connected to this community (including Martha Dodd, Paul and Sylvia Jarrico, and Gale Sondergaard) were actively involved in discussion groups and seminars that focused on the connections between gender, race, and class oppression and the role of culture in perpetuating sexist ideology, and many of them were working to incorporate alternate representations of women into their cultural works.

While living in Mexico City, she wrote *The Lost Traveler* (1958), which provides both a harsh critique of traditional marriage and a model for young women to escape it. The novel is set during the Depression and explores the conflict between Des, a professional gambler, and his independent and willful daughter, Robin. Robin provides a stark contrast to her mother Belle's submissiveness, asserting at one point that she'll never have a husband—only lovers—because she doesn't want to be "bossed around" like her mother (19). When Des tries to cut his wife's hair and give her a stylish new bob, he tells her, "I want you to look like the new, free woman." Robin calls over his shoulder, "*Look* like . . . and *be* the humble wife" (24). Robin has no intention of succumbing to her mother's fate; she plans to run away, get a job, and go to school. Des says of her, "She's as wild as a range filly. . . . I'll have to tame her down" (19).

Throughout the novel, Robin resists the traditional female role her parents try to teach her, and her resistance eventually has a positive effect on both her mother and her father. Later in the novel, Des grows critical of Belle's submissiveness: "By God, didn't she have an ounce of pride? You wouldn't catch Robin doing that" (111). And Belle realizes the dehumanizing nature of their relationship after Des slaps her. She tells him, "You know, Des, I've always been crazy about you, but I don't remember being very happy. I guess you didn't mean to, but I gradually I just got blotted out." When Des tells her she should have stood up for herself, she replies, "I didn't know how" (154). Through Robin, and eventually Belle, Babb's novel provides a model for women in oppressive marriages to stand up for themselves and demand something more.

This thread of women wanting more than just children, home, and family is woven through the works of almost all of the writers discussed thus far. In Lorraine Hansberry's *A Raisin in the Sun*, Beneatha stands against the idea of marriage as the ultimate goal for women. Her dream of being a doctor and her dedication to black nationalism are more important to her than romance. Martha Dodd's unflattering portrayal of Minot's wife, Julia, in *The Searching Light* suggests a critique of the dominant domestic ideology; as in *The Lost Traveler*, the daughter, Lucy, provides a model of a different kind of woman. And Dodd's portrayal of Gertrud and Wolfgang Von Richter, the Nazi couple in *Sowing the Wind*, suggests the profound unhappiness experienced by women who are forced to live out the expectation that women be defined by their relationships to their husbands.

The one fictional character who seems to find an unambiguously supportive partner and a relationship of equals is Mildred, the sassy and militant domestic worker of Alice Childress's *Like One of the Family*. Mildred flat-out rejects the domestic ideology of the age, offering a model of a strong black activist who shows readers how to stand up for themselves and demand justice in both their work and their personal lives. The vignettes in this collection provide a vision of the type of world that readers could create through their activism; Mildred helps readers envision the types of relationships they should strive for. Childress posits Mildred's relationship with Eddie, her traveling salesman partner, as a model for a fulfilling and egalitarian romantic relationship. Mildred often compares him to other men she knows, and these other men fall far short of the mark. In "Dance with Me, Henry," Mildred decides to attend a dance alone, as Eddie is, as usual, on the road. She returns home, dejected because no one asked her to dance, and confides her frustration to Marge: "They're busy pickin' out the glama-rama chicks who got long curlin' hair and shaped like models or something. Or else they expect you to be a ice skatin' champion or a movie star"

(169). This experience allows readers to compare these men to Eddie, who values Mildred for her humor and intelligence, not because she conforms to the dominant image of femininity. Eddie respects her and does not value her for her looks. He makes her laugh, helps with the housework, runs errands for her, and helps her take care of her cousin's children. Additionally, he shares her commitment to the project of promoting black culture. While she emphasizes black women's history, he sells "race-records and books" (223), despite the fact that they are not profitable. Through describing Mildred's relationship with Eddie, Childress encourages her female readers to seek out cooperative relationships based on equality, rather than dependency. And Eddie provides a role model for male readers on how to treat women respectfully.

Other works by Left women writers deal with Communist Party women's efforts to grapple with the nature of commitment and the distribution of housework. Babb's short story "Femme Fatale" (published in *Masses and Mainstream* in 1948) tells the story of an intellectual couple trying to have a nonconventional relationship but struggling with the traditional issue of division of labor. Leslie Dunham and Louise Byrd have been seeing each other for seven years, but neither one wants to consider marriage, for "fear of being bogged down in habitual responsibility and custom" (56). However, despite the freedom they believe their relationship allows them, they still grapple with domestic issues. Although they maintain separate residences, she cooks for him, selects his clothes, and figures out their shared expenses. At times, Louise feels irritated by this arrangement, feeling like she is being exploited. Yet Leslie fails to see or comprehend the unequal division of labor in their relationship. He sparks a recent quarrel by telling her that she is not reading as much as she used to. Even when she tells him she reads less because she cooks more, "while you lie on the couch and read before dinner," her point does not sink in. "But I've just come from work," he tells her, not recognizing that she, too, has just put in a long day at the office (58). The "double duty" of the working-class woman, who had to perform equal labor to her husband on the job and then work a second shift at home, was a common theme among women on the Left. In making Louise a middle-class woman with no children who still struggles with this double duty, Babb shows the pervasiveness of this problem, demonstrating that it is not just a class issue but a gender issue as well.

In addition to critiquing unequal roles in heterosexual relationships, Babb displays the negative effects that societal constructs of beauty and femininity can have on a relationship. Although Louise believes that she values intelligence over beauty, she begins comparing herself to the French heroine in a movie she watches with Leslie. She recognizes that she far outshines the woman in terms of intelligence, but she acknowledges that the woman possesses a beauty and an "ability to maneuver" that she lacks. "Her femininity she thought unfair to use, wanting equality between them. . . . However much she would rather be herself than the heroine, it was apparent that the other had it all over her for attractiveness" (60). Although Louise is critical of society's emphasis on beauty over brains, societal norms still have the power to make her feel insecure—and to question Leslie's devotion to her because she does not live up to those norms.

On the way home from the movie, Louise accuses Leslie of imagining the French girl when he kisses her. He tells her she's wrong: "Seeing a woman like that makes me value you all the more." "I don't care about being *valued*," she tells him. "Of course I do, but I want to be . . . I want to be desired too!" (61). He fails to see the problem she highlights: that mainstream society rewards stereotypically feminine behavior rather than feminine intelligence. Even a woman who is aware of this problem cannot escape it, and, hurt and upset over their earlier quarrel and his failure to understand her current insecurities, she tries to end the relationship. Touched by his concern, she is unable to break it off, and she makes a joke to smooth things over. He laughs in relief and heads to the kitchen to get something to eat. Although he is scared of losing her, he does not take her concerns seriously—nor does he need to. While she is able to identify the "backwardness of the male" (60), she does not try to force him to change or to educate him as to the problems in their relationship, and so nothing changes in the ways they relate to each other.

Often, this unequal division of labor meant that women's domestic duties interfered with their ability to be politically active in the same ways as men. In the year Babb's story was published in *Masses and Mainstream*, debates raged in the pages of the *Worker* about whether women should stay at home or whether they should be supported in their domestic duties so that they could be active politically. Joan Gerson explores some of the complicating factors in couples' efforts to ensure an equal division of labor in "Can a Housewife Be Politically Active?" She wrote, "When our baby was born, my husband and I found ourselves, like so many couples, with a new and bewildering problem to solve: how could both of us continue to be active? In our case that means party activity." She describes how, at first, they divided their activity "down the middle" and occasionally received childcare from her mother-in-law or sister or "worked out an exchange basis with a friend." She says this situation would not have been possible if they had not "approached the situation with a comradely attitude." Her husband seemed to understand that her domestic work was comparable to his paid full-time job, and they worked out an arrangement to share the domestic duties equally so that they both could remain active in the Communist Party. However, a problem emerged when her husband became membership secretary of their branch and she became literature director, as sometimes they would both need to attend meetings. The Party branch worked out an arrangement with a neighborhood youth group to have a college student babysit for them, and this arrangement worked for a while, until husband was transferred to another branch. Without regular childcare, she ended up having to stay home with the children so that he could attend his meetings. The editor added a note at the end of this article, stating, "Mrs. Joan Gerson raises a very serious problem faced by many active women in the labor and progressive movement," and invited readers to share their experiences (Gerson).

Many readers did write in to share their experiences, including Margaret Brill, who wrote about the challenges for her to be involved in Party activities that require her to be out of the house at night: "I am a housewife with two kids, and I'm busy all day along with cooking, cleaning, washing, and taking care of the children. We don't have sufficient money to hire a sitter nights, and my husband refuses to sacrifice some of his time so that I can get out at night." This time, the editor asked readers to respond to some of the specific issues Brill raised. Some of these letters reflect men's failure to recognize that women can make valuable contributions to the struggle, as in Harold B.'s "Fight for Women's Rights Impractical." Harold wrote, "I would be the first to admit that women's position is unenviable. But they are not going to solve their problems by hogtying their husbands. As the breadwinner the man not only has to work during the day, he has to work after hours to protect his job. . . . If this means that his wife is confine[d] to the home, it's tough, but she has to recognize that this is not something he is responsible for." However, just as many letters supported Margaret's position, offering advice on how to share the domestic responsibilities equally, such as "Housewife in Position of Unorganized Worker," signed M. L.: "I insisted that my husband sit down with me not just for a discussion but for a meeting. Before we met I analyzed "my day" and the work for which I had to assume sole responsibility and the work which I felt had to be shared. . . . My husband was forced to recognize the truth of what I said, and we were able to work out a plan that allowed for us sharing our free time."

Two months after these letters appeared, the *Worker* published a special magazine section entitled "We Must Help Women to Become Politically Active." In this section, Margaret Krumbein describes actions the Communist Party took to support women's activism:

In Brooklyn, the Party organized day-time classes for housewives in several sections. Along with the classes, day-nurseries were organized. These nurseries continue after that class is ended. The Party had to provide a budget for this work. The activity of the Communist women in the community where these day-nurseries exist has increased and along with it the activity of other women in the community. . . . While Communist husbands and wives must plan together the division of their time between activities and their home, the Party branch must help in this. In some instances, day-nurseries may be needed. In other cases, the branch should provide sitters for women comrades in important activities. There must be more education by the Party on Marxism and the Woman Question, not only for our women members but for our men comrades as well.

However, this stated commitment to providing childcare for Party mothers did not become a reality for most, thus leaving women to continue to struggle with the unequal distribution of labor.

While the debate raged on in the *Worker* and in discussion groups, *Masses and Mainstream* published several short stories that explored some of the challenges for mothers to be activists. One such story is Margrit Reiner's "The Petition" (1952), which addresses the complex childcare arrangements many women must face in order to become activists. Lois has only an hour to canvass for signatures for a petition against the Korean War (or police action, as it was referred to at the time), as someone else is watching her children. She describes the machinations required to free her to canvass for even an hour:

> Gladys Gregory would take care of Lois' children plus her own, Jane Salzman was watching five kids to free two other mothers for an hour and three teams of husbands and working wives would go out tonight. The small Peace Committee has spent a good three weeks organizing the details of this first attempt at canvassing and the entire membership was involved in one way or another. (44)

Lois was skeptical about her involvement with the Peace Committee to begin with and wonders whether it is worth her time, thinking to herself, "I don't see why women should do this kind of thing, anyway" (44).

However, her perspective changes as she goes from house to house and sees connections between her life and the lives of the other mothers on whose doors she knocks. She also learns by watching the example of her canvassing partner, Mrs. Epstein, a former needle trades worker who has been an activist for several decades; she is a seasoned pro who is no stranger to the challenges that mothers face when trying to work and be an activist at the same time. At every stop, Mrs. Epstein makes a plea for peace to the women as mothers; as she tells one beleaguered mother, "The way I look at it, the mothers should have something to say about war, not the politicians" (45). Lois allows Mrs. Epstein to do most of the talking, until they speak to one woman who tells them she cannot sign the petition because her husband will not allow her to. This woman fits the dominant image of femininity at the time: tied to the home and her children, letting men make big decisions. Lois decides it is time for her to speak up, and she tells her, "I always used to say that—let my husband decide—have to ask my husband. But why, really? If he gets drafted, you suffer just the same. If there's a war, it hurts you just like him. The children are yours and his. Why shouldn't you decide for yourself?" (48). The woman decides to sign it, momentarily resisting the submissive role she is expected to fulfill.

Lois realizes that her failure, up until this point, to act to make the world a better place is an unintended rejection of what her parents tried to teach her: "doing the right thing for others, because one was not alone" (48). Her parents had contributed to antifascist causes, and yet Lois's life changed once she got married and had children. Her priority became her home and family, and her concerns became new curtains and a new electric mixer. But now she realizes that "the way she felt about taking care of her family first and letting the world go its own way had hurt somebody. . . . It had hurt her and Jack and the children and the country, for if it happened to her it had happened to others and here was a war knocking at their doors and they didn't know why" (49). She realizes that in order to be a good wife and mother, she needs to be thinking about the world beyond her home, and that her activism is actually a way for her to be a good wife and mother.

The connection between motherhood and activism is one that is also explored in the work of Anna Seghers (the pseudonym of Netty Radvány), a German novelist and Left-wing intellectual whose writings were prohibited in Germany when Hitler came to power; she was driven into exile to avoid further persecution. Seghers's short story "The Delegate's Daughter" (*Masses and Mainstream*, 1952) is set in Poland, under the dictatorship of Marshal Pilsudski, and addresses building a new society from a mother's perspective. Even though the Communist Party had been banned in Poland, Party meetings were held in secret. Felka (the delegate of the title) is a reticent woman who emerges as strike leader and is chosen as a delegate to the trade union congress in Moscow. However, to attend the meeting she must leave behind her eleven-year-old daughter, Jozia. When her arranged childcare falls through (the family members who were supposed to watch Jozia come down with scarlet fever, and the close friends who then agree to watch her are arrested), Felka makes the difficult decision to leave Jozia alone, and much of the story focuses on the daughter's struggle without her mother. The story raises the issue of the importance of childcare for women to be able to participate fully in resistance movements. It also challenges the idea that the way to be a good woman is to be tied to the home, family, and children. Felka worries about Jozia constantly while she is away, but she also thinks of the better world she is working to build. This lesson is not lost on Jozia, who grows up to become an activist in the resistance movement herself.

Other Left writers from this era sought to provide role models for young girls like Jozia, representations of women that challenged the domestic ideology. Adolescent coming-of-age novels such as Jo Sinclair's *The Changelings* (1955) and Paule Marshall's *Brown Girl, Brownstones* (1959) show the development of class, race, and gender consciousness within working-class communities. Marshall, who had been a member of the American Youth for Democracy (a successor to the Young Communist League), set her novel within the Barbadian immigrant community in Brooklyn. Selina Boyce, the female protagonist of Marshall's novel, rejects the middle-class values that her mother and the rest of her community embrace. The novel traces Selina's path from individual development and conflict with her community's values to a recognition of her connections to the black community, especially to the women within it. This recognition helps her to see the necessity of acting out of a consciousness of her position in an oppressed group, rather than as an isolated individual. While she has not yet figured out how she will become politically involved, her awareness of the need for solidarity suggests the beginnings of a revolutionary consciousness. Similarly, in *The Changelings*, Judith Vincent (an outsider because she is Jewish, working class, and a girl) rejects her parents' racist values after she strikes up a friendship with Clara (an outsider because she is black, working class, and a girl). In the course of the novel, Vincent learns that solidarity can be an important mode of survival. Sinclair, an antifascist writer who contributed to *New Masses* and other Party publications in the 1930s, ends her novel on an optimistic note, with Vincent (as she prefers to be called) feeling "the whole world opening in front of her as she ran. In a moment, she could touch it" (322). Like Selina, Vincent has not yet become an activist, but the novel's ending implies that her newfound awareness of the importance of interracial solidarity opens up possibilities for creating a better world. Both novels offered inspiration to young women that they could seek different paths from their families and work for social change.

Women writers on the Left also sought to provide young women with strong female role models through biographies of inspirational feminist foremothers. Dorothy Sterling claims that she wrote *Freedom Train: The Story of Harriet Tubman* (1954) because she wanted "to write a biography of a woman, a heroic figure who would say to girls, 'You are as strong and capable as boys'" ("Four Score" 139). Ann Petry also wrote a biography of Harriet Tubman during this time, and Shirley Graham wrote one on Phillis Wheatley. Childress's *Like One of the Family* has several vignettes that address the value of teaching young people about Tubman and Sojourner Truth, but she also emphasizes the importance of educating young women about black women's unsung contributions to the survival of the black family.

And other writers strove to provide role models for all women through the stories of antifascist fighters. In a column encouraging women readers to join the Communist Party, Meridel Le Sueur gives several examples of women "comrades" in other countries: "So often I think of the Communist women in the world whose warm humanity and fighting spirit sustained the underground of occupied countries, who fought invaders with bombs in their market baskets, and guns in their hands, and it's a steady thing to think that they are everywhere alive, warm, great mothers, wives, friends and comrades" ("You" 11). Her column is accompanied by sketches of women activists in Spain, Italy, Romania, and the Soviet Union.

Masses and Mainstream published several short stories by authors who featured model antifascist fighters. One author is Renata Vigano, who wrote about women's involvement in the Italian resistance movement during World War II.[2] Vigano had firsthand experience in the resistance; her husband was a commander in the Garibaldi Brigades, and she joined him in the struggle, along with their baby son. Her novel, *Agnes Is Going to Die* (1949), tells the story of the Italian resistance through Agnes, an elderly peasant woman. *Masses and Mainstream* published an excerpt from this novel in 1954. Another example is Margrit Reiner's short story "Morning," which also explores the issues of the power of solidarity between women. Published in *Masses and Mainstream* in March 1951, Reiner's story shows women in their roles as mothers find their own ways to fight back against Nazi power. Reiner was living in New York at the time the story was published but was originally from Vienna, which was under Nazi rule from 1938 to 1945. The story is set during the Nazi occupation; it opens with Anni, who has been in a feverish state for several days, awakening to learn that she has lost her baby and that her husband (a member of the resistance movement) has had to flee. She is the good hands of Marie, a neighbor woman whom she barely knows. Anni feels hopeless as she remembers the loss of her unborn child at the hands of a Nazi officer with "thin lips and hard eyes" (49) and tells Marie that she wishes she were dead.

Marie, on the other hand, refuses to let her feel defeated. She tells her about the strength of other women and the ways they have found to participate in the resistance. "Now take Watzek's Gretl," she tells Anni. "Three kids and her man in jail. That's enough to get anyone down. But not her." Marie goes on to describe how Gretl obtains the membership list for her husband's platoon and sends her son to warn them (51). Marie also tells Anni about Martha Kressner, an elderly neighbor who did everything she could to prevent her son from joining the resistance. When her son is killed by the Nazis, however, she has a change of heart, and becomes involved in helping those poor kids who've lost their fathers" (51).

After hearing these stories, and recognizing Marie's own courage in caring for her, Anni realizes that the loss of her child to Nazi violence means she has to take a stand against fascism. "We'll have to do something about the families," she tells Marie. "The families of the victims" (52). Marie nods, and the two women form a bond in their grief, a bond that will allow them to fight for the families of other victims of Nazi violence. This moment of solidarity echoes the scene in the butter shop in *Sowing the Wind*, as well as the ring of lanterns in *The Drinking Gourd*, showing that women found support and strength through each other.

As women and men on the Left struggled to articulate and define a vision of a more just and equal world, the issue of romantic and domestic relationships presented a constant stumbling block. The frustration and disappointment reflected in these literary works demonstrates the tensions and conflicts created by this gap between theory and lived reality. These issues would be taken up once again in the consciousness-raising groups of the 1960s and 1970s, with powerful results. However, some of these works also present alternatives to the prevailing domestic ideology, encourage solidarity between women, and provide hope that all women are not passively accepting traditional marriage roles or otherwise succumbing to the feminine mystique. Despite the repressive domestic ideology of the McCarthy era, many women on the Left were seeking to redefine their relationships and make the personal political.

Epilogue

A Left Feminist Literary History

The literary works I have recovered for this project clearly attest to a vibrant and important Left feminist culture in the postwar era. However, I by no means mean to imply that the postwar era was a heyday for women on the Left. The pervasive political repression of the McCarthy era was very real and very damaging; the repercussions are still felt to this day. The crusade against un-American activity was not limited to Communist Party leaders and activists; it also extended to Left-wing cultural workers. In 1947, the House Un-American Activities Committee (HUAC) began investigating the Hollywood branch of the Party, charging that filmmakers were planting subversive messages in movies. The first ten screenwriters summoned before HUAC refused to testify. The Hollywood Ten, as they came to be called, were all cited for contempt and sentenced to jail. Hundreds of other writers, directors, and actors were blacklisted.[1] In order to continue their work, some screenwriters wrote under pseudonyms or used "fronts," the practice of using a surrogate to take credit for a script written by a blacklistee. Others left the country, while many never found work.

The blacklist also extended to other areas of the entertainment industry. In 1950, a group of former FBI agents published *Red Channels*, a list of over 150 television and radio performers and their Communist affiliations; it became a de facto blacklist. As in Hollywood, it destroyed the careers of many of the entertainers listed within its pages. In *Scoundrel Time* (1976), her memoir of the McCarthy era, writer Lillian Hellman, who was summoned before HUAC in 1952, writes that the committee's research director told her lawyer that "they were doing the 'entire entertainment field' and were particularly interested in the 'literary field' to show how the Communist Party sought to control the thinking of its members" (88). Many writers with Left ties had trouble publishing, as agents and editors refused to take chances on writers who could be perceived as dangerous. Meridel Le Sueur, for example, struggled to find publishing venues and had difficulty surviving financially after being named by HUAC. According to Constance Coiner, the family was under constant FBI surveillance and had trouble keeping jobs. Le Sueur, who had published frequently with mainstream presses in the 1920s and 1930s, found herself blacklisted by most major publishing houses.[2] While she was able to publish children's books, many public libraries banned these books because of what one newspaper review referred to as their "pink-tinged" pages (Schleuning 109). These books provided some income, but Le Sueur managed to eke out a meager existence during this period primarily by running a boardinghouse and teaching creative writing classes. However, even this source of income was limited, as the FBI effectively frightened off many of her students and boarders (Coiner 82–83). It is no wonder that Le Sueur referred to this period as "the dark of the time" (*Ripening* 231).

Former Communist Party member and writer Dorothy Sterling recalls having a manuscript rejected abruptly by several publishing houses, even though they originally showed an interest in it. Years later, when she obtained her FBI file through the Freedom of Information Act, she found a memo from the FBI's assistant director, warning a publisher (whose name had been blacked out) that "[they] should be very careful about what they did about Dorothy Sterling" (personal interview). Sterling was able to find work writing children's books, as was Le Sueur, while other writers were able to publish through Party presses. Myra Page (who taught the first class on the Woman Question at the Jefferson School) began her novel *Daughter of the Hills* (1950) in the late 1930s and completed it shortly after World War II. While she had signed a contract with Viking Press, it returned her contract after she had been named as a Communist. A group of her friends on the Left raised money to publish the novel with Citadel Press (Rosenfelt, Afterword 247). So while the Left culture industry was not destroyed, it was severely hampered. Scores of Left writers became part of what Laura Hapke refers to as the "literary underground of silenced, culturally invisible proletarian writers" (265).

All in all, the McCarthy-era campaign against the Left had repercussions for thousands of people. Ellen Schrecker assesses the effects of the anticommunist crusade on the activists, writers, teachers, musicians, and artists who supported the Communist Party. "There was, to begin with," she writes, "a lot of human wreckage" (*Many* 360). Scores of professors and government workers lost their jobs for their refusals to sign loyalty oaths. Marriages, families, and friendships were destroyed. Almost everyone targeted suffered some form of mental and physical duress, and several people committed suicide. Many left the country, either to find work or to escape possible imprisonment. An exile community in Mexico included Party leaders, members of the Hollywood Ten, and several artists and writers, including Martha Dodd, Sanora Babb, Albert Maltz, Dalton Trumbo, Gordon Kahn, Hugo and Jean (Rouverol) Butler, Howard Fast, John Bright, Julian Zimet, and Elizabeth Catlett.[3] The cost to careers and relationships was high for most of the individuals involved, and a number of important oppositional voices were silenced.

Schrecker concedes that most of the people targeted by the anticommunist crusade were, in fact, involved with the Communist Party. However, she insists that, while many Party members did follow the Soviet Party line, and while some were, in fact, spies for the Soviet Union, the majority of people targeted were under attack for their connections to pro-Communist antiracist, antifascist, and labor organizations, rather than for their support of a violent overthrow of the government. Indeed, she views Communism in the United States as more of a movement, a movement she describes as "both subservient to the Kremlin and genuinely dedicated to a wide range of social reforms, a movement whose adherents sometimes toed the party line and sometimes did not even receive it" (*Many* xiii). Alan Wald's extensive research on Communist cultural activity in the United States supports this position. He argues in "The Costs of McCarthyism":

> What made one part of the Communist movement, formally or informally, was always a personal conviction that the Party and Moscow stood almost alone against fascism, racism and exploitation. Thus an ordinary Party supporter who aided the international movement did not necessarily think of himself or herself as "subversive" to the United States, but of demonstrating the highest expression of genuine patriotism and loyalty to all humanity. (32)

Yet such "patriots" were accused of being un-American and most paid a heavy price for their disloyalty.

As part of my research for this book, I requested several FBI files under the Freedom of Information/Privacy Acts. Alice Childress's FBI file perhaps gave me the fullest picture of the extent to which culture was used in the service of the movement, while also revealing the level of surveillance against those suspected of being Communists. Childress's file shows that she led songs at Party meetings, organized cultural events for May Day and "Negro History month" celebrations, staged musical reviews of African American and Jewish American women's history, and planned cultural events at Camp Unity, an adult pro-Communist resort. These acts are hardly threatening (let alone treasonous), and yet she was followed and had many of her activities recorded. Her actions were nothing to be ashamed of, yet these experiences clearly had a negative impact on Childress, making her reluctant to claim her Left past. Kathy Perkins, who designed the lighting for one of Childress's plays and knew her for the last ten years of her life, told me, "For the most part she did not like to discuss too much regarding her past. She was very selective in what she wanted to discuss."

McCarthyism has shaped Americans' perceptions of Communists as enemies of the freedom, democracy, and individual rights supposedly inherent in American society. It has also distorted former Communists' perceptions of themselves, and many writers and activists associated with the Old Left of the 1930s, 1940s, and 1950s have disavowed or are fearful to discuss their pasts. As a result, the social movements of the 1960s are often viewed as disconnected from any previous tradition of resistance. Perhaps the most striking example of this phenomenon is that of Betty Friedan. Friedan is widely recognized as one of the founding mothers of feminism's second wave. Her presentation of herself in *The Feminine Mystique* (1963) as an unhappy homemaker, bored with her domestic suburban lifestyle, tapped into the feelings of discontent shared by many white, middle-class women throughout the United States. Friedan's work has come under attack as focusing too narrowly on the concerns of white, middle-class, married women and ignoring the struggles of working-class women and women of color. It is surprising, then, to learn through Daniel Horowitz's research that she had previously had connections to the United Electrical, Radio and Machine Workers of America (UE), a radical labor union committed to women's rights. While Friedan completely disavows this Left past and reinvents herself as a middle-class housewife in *The Feminine Mystique*, many of the ideas in this work are deeply rooted in the Left's critique of domestic ideology in the 1940s and 1950s. In one section, Friedan uses the concept of the fascist triple K to describe the domestic ideology championed by women's magazines. Her critiques of books and magazines bear a strong resemblance to those in the *Worker* and *Masses and Mainstream*. And she devotes a significant amount of space to discussing *Modern Woman: The Lost Sex*, using language that echoes the 1940s critiques of the book made by Party leaders Claudia Jones, Elizabeth Gurley Flynn, and William Z. Foster.

Although Friedan made every effort to deny it, these similarities are not coincidental; they can be directly traced to Friedan's involvement in the Old Left. While many feminist historians credit *The Feminine Mystique* with starting the modern feminist movement, Horowitz's work makes a powerful case for this movement, and Friedan's book, being rooted in the ideas and struggles of the Old Left. As he puts it, "social movements and their leaders do not . . . come out of nowhere. They have histories that powerfully shape their destinies" (*Betty* 245). While understanding Friedan's past provides an entirely new lens through which to view the modern women's movement, Friedan made every effort to distance herself from Horowitz's research. In the final years of her life, rather than acknowledging the source of many of the ideas in her groundbreaking book, she attempted to maintain the image of herself that she constructed in *The Feminine Mystique*. The majority of obituaries printed after her death in 2006 would suggest that she was largely successful in upholding this image.[4]

In contrast to Friedan, historian Gerda Lerner chose to embrace her Left past in *Fireweed: A Political Autobiography* (2002).[5] Lerner, a pioneering scholar of women's history, is candid about her involvement with the Communist Party and claims that her attention to race, class, and gender as a historian "comes directly out of my life and experience." She writes, "I could never have written and edited *Black Women in White America: A Documentary History* (1972) . . . if it had not been for my experiences" in the Left (*Fireweed* 371). Eleanor Flexner, author of *Century of Struggle* (1959), the classic history of the women's suffrage movement, acknowledges a similar debt. When interviewed later in life, she stated, "I can definitely trace the origins of my book to some of my contacts with Communists like Elizabeth Gurley Flynn and Claudia Jones" (qtd. in Rosen 33). By being unrepentant about her Left past, Lerner acknowledges the debt that she and other feminists owe to the Old Left.

As in the field of women's history, many of the seminal texts in postwar US women's literature are rooted in the ideas of the Old Left. And US feminist literary history provides glimpses into this relationship. For example, Tillie Olsen's *Silences* (1978) is widely credited with opening the study of literature to women and working-class writers. Olsen freely admitted that her ideas were grounded in her experience within the Left.[6] Audre Lorde's *Zami*, her autobiography of growing up as an African American lesbian in the 1950s, is a staple of women's studies courses, but it could also be read as a primer in Left culture during the McCarthy era. Lorde lived with a Party activist, belonged to the Harlem Writers Guild, and fled to Mexico to escape the repressive atmosphere of the McCarthy era; she chronicles these events, as well as the Left's homophobia and persecution of gay people, in *Zami*. Grace Paley's roots in the Communist Party in the 1930s and her legacy of radicalism influenced her short stories exploring women's experiences, beginning with her collection *The Little Disturbances of Man* (1959).

And then there is the generation of young black female writers who published in *Freedomways*, the successor to Robeson's *Freedom*, which was established in 1961 with the goal of continuing *Freedom*'s tradition of a progressive black cultural journal. According to James Smethurst, *Freedomways* cofounder Louis Burnham "saw it as a place where older artists, such as Alice Childress, John Oliver Killens, Lorraine Hansberry, W.E.B. Du Bois, Shirley Graham Du Bois, Margaret Burroughs, and others who had been part of the *Freedom* circle . . . could reach out to a new audience, especially among the younger militants, after being isolated (and in some cases exiled) by McCarthyism" ("SNYC" 8). In addition to works by these writers and artists with roots in the Old Left, the journal printed the work of younger black artists, such as Audre Lorde, Paule Marshall, Nikki Giovanni, Alice Walker, and June Jordan. Smethurst's research makes a strong case for *Freedomways* as a bridge between the Old Left of the 1930s, '40s, and '50s and the Black Arts Movement, as well as a model for a new generation of black radicals.

But works by these authors provide just glimpses into the relationship between the Old Left, feminism, and postwar literary culture. McCarthyism severely hampered the careers of hundreds of other Left cultural workers, relegating many of them to obscurity (or, in the case of Childress, Hansberry, and others, erasing their Left past). Rescuing these works from their Cold War exile and analyzing them in the context of postwar Left feminism helps to rewrite US feminist literary history in a way that acknowledges a continuous tradition of resistance, a tradition that has largely been erased by the red-baiting of the McCarthy era. In her biography of her labor activist parents (written shortly after their deaths), Meridel Le Sueur discusses the need to resurrect the culture of past movements. In one particularly compelling passage, she describes funerals as a means

> of conveying history that has become hidden, of subtly informing the young, and of mining and blowing the mineral of collective poetry and courage. . . . In these memorials a pattern is made which can be followed by others. This is a collective history told by people who lived it. Memory in America suffers amnesia. Here the memory is blown from the ashes and glows in the city. (*Crusaders* 63–64)

Le Sueur wrote these words in 1955 when, despairing over the repression of the McCarthy era, she looked to the past to reclaim her parents' legacy of resistance. Le Sueur's words serve as a reminder of the importance of looking to the past for usable lessons. However, it is the words of Alice Childress, Martha Dodd, Lorraine Hansberry, Claudia Jones, Thelma Dale, Sanora Babb, Beth McHenry, and the many other writers I was fortunate to uncover that remind me to work toward creating a vision of what the future can be.

Notes

INTRODUCTION

1. In "Cold War Revisions: Representation and Resistance in the Unseen *Salt of the Earth*," Benjamin Balthaser argues that this process of revision actually diluted the strength of the film's original, intended critique of anti-communism, imperialism, and the Korean War. While his analysis of the preproduction draft gives strength to this argument, I still believe that the film is a powerful critique of the existing domestic ideology and a groundbreaking representation of women's issues and political participation.

2. Rosenfelt also notes that Sylvia Jarrico (wife of the film's producer) was writing feminist film criticism and actress Gale Sondergaard (wife of the film's director) did a one-woman Marxist-feminist show in the 1950s. See her Commentary 107.

3. In *Women and the American Left*, Mari Jo Buhle defines the "Woman Question" as "How could women make claims on behalf of the liberation of their sex and simultaneously, and with equal commitment, advance the struggles of the working class? In other words, what was the categorical relationship of class and gender in theories, strategies, and practices of social change?" (viii).

4. I use the term "Left feminist" (rather than Marxist feminist or socialist feminist) to connote more of an activist stance than a theoretical one.

5. Before beginning this project, I had thought of Left culture as transmitting a certain agenda, and, indeed, many people tend to think of Left culture as nothing more than propaganda. My research has helped me see the important role that culture played in building and maintaining community, in creating an alternative culture that reflected the vision of a socialist future that most Party members wanted to create. Although people might have differed on what that future looked like, most people involved with the Communist Party shared the belief that socialism was the best way to create an egalitarian society—and that culture was a way of helping to envision that society, to propel it in that direction.

6. See also Alan Wald's discussion of premature socialist-feminists in his *Exiles from a Future Time* (252–61); Michael Denning's discussion in his *The Cultural Front* of the "rank-and-file 'left feminism'" that existed during the Popular Front years (136–38); and Barbara Foley's "Women and the Left in the 1930s" in her *Radical Representations*.

7. For several decades after it was produced, only a few copies of the film remained in print. The release of a VHS version in the early 1990s and a DVD version in 1999 helped the film gain a wider audience, as did the national conference celebrating the film, held at the College of Santa Fe in February 2003.

8. While the mainstream culture industry of the postwar era defined femininity as finding contentment in the role of wife, mother, and homemaker, several key texts challenge this domestic ideology. In *Homeward Bound: American Families in the Cold War Era* (1999), Elaine Tyler May argues that this domestic ideology developed alongside the Cold War and that women who did not fit the image of the white, middle-class, heterosexual, married mother and homemaker were considered threats to a stable society. In *The Way We Never Were: American Families and the Nostalgia Trap* (1992), Stephanie Coontz shows that the mainstream image of family and femininity was only a reality for

a minority of Americans in the 1950s. Joanne Meyerowitz's *Not June Cleaver: Women and Gender in Postwar America, 1945–1960* (1994) considers the experiences of working-class women, women of color, lesbians, immigrant women, and feminist activists; this collection of essays provides case studies of feminist activism in labor, peace, and other progressive organizations.

9. While the history of women on the Left in the 1940s and '50s is just beginning to be written, very few studies exist that address Left literature from the postwar era. Alan Wald's "Marxist Literary Resistance to the Cold War" (1996) lays out a map of writers whose Left pasts are waiting to be uncovered; a forthcoming work will focus on the literary Left in the Cold War era. Mary Helen Washington's "Alice Childress, Lorraine Hansberry, and Claudia Jones: Black Women Write the Popular Front" (2003) argues that both feminist and African American literary histories have largely overlooked Childress's roots in the 1950s Left. And Kevin Gaines's "From Center to Margin: Internationalism and the Origins of Black Feminism" mentions black feminist foresight in the works of Childress, Hansberry, and Gwendolyn Brooks. However, no comprehensive study of Left feminist culture during this era exists. This book is the first to tell this largely neglected story.

CHAPTER 1

1. Scholars vary in their usage of terms to describe this era in US history. Many use the term "Cold War," but as the Cold War extended until the fall of the Soviet Union, I believe a more historically specific term is necessary to delimit the 1940s and 1950s. Others use the term "postwar" to describe the period from the end of World War II through 1960. While this time period roughly covers the same era, the term does not necessarily convey the anticommunist hysteria that characterized the political climate. Thus, I use the terms "McCarthyism" and "McCarthy era" to describe this time period.

2. The anticommunist crusade that permeated American life during these years was not the first such campaign against the Left in the United States. Business leaders and factory owners had viewed communism as a threat since the 1917 Russian Revolution. Fearful of labor unrest, business leaders (and the politicians they supported) spread anticommunist propaganda throughout the United States, depicting communism as a threat to the American way of life and using anticommunism as a justification to arrest labor activists and other radicals and to deport immigrants. However, anticommunist repression reached new levels during the early years of the Cold War.

3. According to Leila Haber, these three magazines had a combined circulation of thirteen million in 1953. See "A Look at the Big 3 in Women's Magazines," *Sunday Worker* 27 Dec. 1953: 8.

4. Articles in Ingram's defense appeared frequently in the *Worker*, and *Masses and Mainstream* published several poems honoring Ingram's courage and strength, including Eve Merriam's "Spring Cleaning" (1952) and Lucy Smith's "The Lesson" (1954).

5. Given the Communist Party's treatment of lesbians, as described by Audre Lorde in her autobiography *Zami*, it is no wonder that these women stayed in the closet. Lorde claims homosexuality was "outside the party line at that time." Her roommate, Rhea, who was active in Left circles, was "denounced for her association" with Lorde and ostracized for keeping "such questionable company in 1955" (Lorde 195, 198).

CHAPTER 2

1. While Dodd and her husband were cleared on all counts in 1979, due to lack of evidence, various sources have since suggested that perhaps there was some truth to the charges. Weinstein and Vassiliev's *The Haunted Wood: Soviet Espionage in America—the Stalin Era* (1999) charges that Dodd was most definitely spying for the Soviet Union, based on Weinstein's temporary and exclusive access to the Stalin-era files of the NKVD (the Soviet intelligence agency and predecessor to the KGB). Further, in *Venona: Decoding Soviet Espionage in America* (1999), John Earl Haynes and Harvey Klehr indict Dodd (along with several hundred other Americans) as a Soviet spy, based on the Venona files, a series of Soviet cables intercepted and decoded by US intelligence agents in the 1930s and '40s. However, the accuracy of the materials in both the Venona and the NKVD files has been the subject of considerable debate. Many historians have argued that the content of both the NKVD and Venona files is unverifiable. Weinstein has come under fire for his failure to follow the accepted scholarly standards of openness. His publisher paid for exclusive access to the NKVD files, and Weinstein has not allowed anyone else to see the archival materials he and Vassiliev draw on in *The Haunted Wood*. When Weinstein was nominated to be the archivist of the United States (a position he held from 2005 to 2008), nineteen organizations, including the Society of American Archivists and the Organization of American Historians, issued a joint statement expressing concern about his nomination on ethical grounds. Even those who agree with his conclusions, such as Whittaker Chambers's biographer Sam Tanenhaus, have been critical of Weinstein's methods, particularly his failure to document his archival sources properly. Further, the accuracy of the Venona files has also been called into question. The intercepted cables use code names to refer to the individuals involved, and the activities described therein have been attributed to specific individuals, without verification that these individuals were the ones who actually committed the activities described. Klehr and Haynes rely on these uncorroborated attributions as proof; additionally, they leave out evidence that might absolve the individuals they indict. As historian Ellen Schrecker writes in *Many Are the Crimes: McCarthyism in America* (1998), "There are too many gaps in the record to use these materials with complete confidence" (xvii–xviii).

2. At present, no scholarly work has been done on Dodd as a literary figure. Alan Wald has acknowledged that Dodd's life and work would make her an "excellent candidate for revival," but otherwise, cultural histories of both feminism and the Left fail to include her. See Wald, *Writing* 21. However, with the recent publication of a German edition of Dodd's memoir, *Through Embassy Eyes*, by Frankfurt-based publisher Eichborn Verlag, it is possible that her literary works will begin to receive more attention.

3. Dodd came to appreciate both men's integrity and their sense of the need for artists to be concerned with injustice. She dedicated her first novel to Lovett (and her husband) and continued to turn to him for creative advice.

4. According to press clippings in the Dodd papers, she had been secretly engaged before marrying Roberts but had broken off the marriage. For more information about Dodd's marriage to Roberts, as well as about her many alleged affairs, see Erik Larson's *In the Garden of the Beasts: Love, Terror, and an American Family in Hitler's Berlin* (2011).

5. Officially a party from 1936 to 1956, the American Labor Party (ALP) originally forwarded a pro-Left but non-Socialist platform. Communists quickly gained control of the ALP and, by 1941, had driven away the liberal Left wing. While clearly a party that fought for working-class interests, the ALP also prioritized antiracism and antifascism. See Isserman, *Which Side*; Meyer, "American."

6. See Aaron; Denning; Foley; and Wald, *Exiles*.

7. Erik Larson claims that Landt's character was based on one of Dodd's former lovers, Ernst Udet, a famous German flying ace from World War I (113, 359).

8. Sylvia Crane tells this story in her comments at Alfred's memorial service in 1986. When the Sterns were charged with espionage, Crane was among those interviewed by the FBI about the Sterns's Communist involvement and was later subpoenaed by HUAC to testify about their activities.

9. *Through Embassy Eyes* was a best-seller upon its publication and was reprinted on the day it was issued; it went through four printings in its first month.

10. The *New York Times* described it as "challenging to the mind" (Mitgang); the *St. Louis Post Dispatch* claimed that "by spreading understanding about the real threat to the democratic way of life" represented by "the shameful incidents" in the novel, it "may help to prevent their recurrence" (Aldridge); the *Nation* described it as "a true mirror image of the United States today," based on "an honest commitment to freedom and truth" (Feuchtwanger); the *National Guardian* reviewer wrote that *The Searching Light*'s "powerful lessons" make it "one of the very important novels of 1955," one that "deserves the widest reading" (Citron).

11. Albert Maltz, the radical novelist and dramatist and member of the Hollywood Ten, described the novel as "a substantial contribution to the literature of the American scene in the era of the Cold War." Annette Rubinstein (vice-chair of the New York Peace Association) wrote that *The Searching Light* is not only a "good novel," but one that can "deepen the understanding and strengthen the determination of those who . . . already know that nothing which is happening in the world about us is truly apart from themselves" (63).

12. In a 1949 article on university loyalty oaths, published in *Masses and Mainstream*, Samuel Sillen discusses several cases in which professors with otherwise unblemished academic records were fired. While a few of these professors belonged to the Communist Party, he argues that most were targeted because of their association with antiracist or antifascist struggles ("Behind").

13. In a postscript written for the Czech edition of the novel, Dodd compares Penfield's climate to the fascism she witnessed in Nazi Germany: "Unfortunately, a great number of Americans, like a great number of Germans before them under Hitler, plagued by anxieties about their economic security and their future in this atomic age, have been psychologically prepared to blame any minority, like the Communists, the Jews or the Negroes for their sterile uncertain life and therefore fall easy prey to the vicious propaganda of the hate-mongers who are now in control of national life."

14. Dodd was an admirer of the work of David Alfara Siqueiros, a revolutionary Mexican painter whose artwork and activism prioritized the plight of the worker and the inevitability of revolution, and the Communist muralist Diego Rivera. Siqueiros was jailed in Mexico City for his activities as an organizer of workers, artists, and intellectuals. Dodd tried to raise awareness of his plight in her 1961 article, "Imprison a Flame," published in the Sunday *Worker* and in China, Cuba, and several European newspapers. She compared Siqueiros's arrest to the HUAC witch hunts, criticizing "the

fantastic and ridiculous charge of 'social dissolution'" levied against him "as alarmingly vague and in-clusive of vast illegal application as is the term 'subversive' in the USA." She attributes this spread to pressure from the US government, or what she refers to as "the 'frightened giant'" at the US-Mexico border. In drawing attention to Siqueiros's situation in this essay and in "Prisoner #4678860" (pub-lished two years later in the *Worker*), Dodd calls attention to the growing threat of anticommunism for political activists and cultural workers throughout the world. Siqueiros became a hero of sorts to the Left. Pablo Neruda wrote a poem about him, and Lorraine Hansberry signed a petition calling for his release.

15. For information on the Left feminist politics of the Hollywood Left, see Rosenfelt, Com-mentary 107, 159. Dodd's letters also indicate close friendships with Ring Lardner, Albert Maltz, and Dalton Trumbo.

CHAPTER 3

1. The Mildred columns were also reprinted in the *Baltimore Afro-American* after they were com-piled into the *Like One of the Family* collection. Childress wrote several entirely new columns for the *Afro-American*, a weekly publication that encouraged blacks to organize for racial and economic equality.

2. The biographical information in this paragraph comes from this essay and Jennings, *Alice Chil-dress*.

3. See Naison, *Communists in Harlem during the Depression*; Maxwell, *New Negro, Old Left: African-American Writing and Communism between the Wars*; Kelley, *Hammer and Hoe: Alabama Communists during the Great Depression*.

4. Pitts's dissertation provides one of the few in-depth studies of the ANT.

5. See *Daily Worker* 22 Feb. 1950: 8; *Daily Worker* 3 Apr. 1951: 5.

6. Although *Gold through the Trees* is clearly an important Childress work, the script was never published and Childress did not register it with the Copyright Division at the Library of Congress.

7. See *Daily Worker* 6 Aug. 1950: 7.

8. My discussion of the play uses Childress's original, preferred ending, published in Patterson.

9. Other writers on the Left shared this desire. In the introduction to *Native Son* (1940), Richard Wright claims that he wanted to write a protest novel that white audiences could not cry over as they had with his earlier collection of stories, *Uncle Tom's Children* (1938). He did not like that white audiences could feel good because they felt bad for the poor black characters, and, after reading the reviews for that book, he "swore . . . that if [he] ever wrote another book, no one would weep over it; that it would be so hard and deep that they would have to face it without the consolation of tears" (xxvii).

10. In the introduction to the 1986 reprint, Harris claims, "Whatever the reason, *Like One of the Family*—as near as I have been able to uncover—was reviewed only once in the four years following its publication" (xxvii).

11. When I taught selections from *Like One if the Family* in a literature course, my students agreed with Harris's assessment. Many of them referred to Mildred as a black superwoman; and they were all surprised and encouraged to read that a black woman from this era had been so outspoken.

12. Childress based her 1950 musical review, *Just a Little Simple*, on these stories.

13. In the introduction to *Like One of the Family*, Trudier Harris claims that Childress's refusal to give Mildred "middle-class embellishments" was "unlike anything preceding it in "Afro-American literature." She goes on to say that "Mildred breaks the mold of casting black women as alien to or bemoaning their experiences in order to make them acceptable to white audiences" (xxix–xxx). In other words, black women needed to fit the demeaning stereotypes or else ape a white, middle-class lifestyle.

14. Also reprinted (in slightly altered form) as "Story Tellin' Time" in *Like One of the Family*.

CHAPTER 4

1. Hansberry also replaced the lead female character with a man in *The Sign in Sidney Brustein's Window*. In a *New York Times* article, Hansberry mentions that she began writing this play about a female friend who had been harassed because she had a political poster in her window, but "Jenny Reed" turned into "Sidney Brustein," a white intellectual who has lost his faith in social movements ("Village" 2:1).

2. Several key recent studies explore Hansberry's ties to this community: Mary Helen Washington's "Alice Childress, Lorraine Hansberry, and Claudia Jones: Black Women Write the Popular Front," Kevin Gaines's "From Center to Margin: Internationalism and the Origins of Black Feminism," Dayo Gore's *Radicalism at the Crossroads: African American Women Activists in the Cold War*, and Erik S. McDuffie's *Sojourning for Freedom: Black Women, American Communism, and the Making of Black Left Feminism*.

3. Much of Hansberry's critical reputation derives from her success as the playwright of *A Raisin in the Sun*. When the play opened on Broadway in 1959, it became an immediate hit, earning Hansberry the New York Drama Critics Circle Award and a contract with Columbia Pictures for the movie rights. How Hansberry became the first black woman to have a play produced on Broadway, despite her outspoken and unapologetic radical politics, and despite the fact that she had been under FBI surveillance for her Communist ties dating back to 1948, is a mystery. Even though many of the more controversial aspects of the play were toned down or cut out altogether, I have to wonder how the movie made it to Broadway at all, given that most artists in this era who were suspected of having even the slightest Left-wing ties were censored or blacklisted. But the FBI made no efforts to interfere with production, and the play was widely attended.

4. A Communist Party member and longtime black activist, Burnham had been involved with the Southern Negro Youth Congress since the early 1940s and had served as the southern director of the Progressive Party. Hansberry credits him with teaching her much about journalism as a form of activism. In *To Be Young, Gifted, and Black*, Hansberry remembers, "The things he taught me were great things: that all racism was rotten, white or black, that *everything* is political; that people tend to be indescribably beautiful and uproariously funny. He also taught me that they have enemies who are grotesque and that freedom lies in the recognition of all that and other things" (99–100).

5. According to Mary Helen Washington, Hansberry and Jones either lived together or lived in the same building (personal interview 15 Aug. 2001).

6. Hansberry wrote this essay for *The Fair Sex*, a magazine that was intended as an intellectual women's counterpart to *Mademoiselle* but never got off the ground.

7. *The Ladder* began as the newsletter for the Daughters of Bilitis, a San Francisco–based lesbian organization. At the time, no publications specifically for lesbians existed, and many writers contributed for free (although some, like Hansberry, wrote under pseudonyms). It was published from October 1956 through August/September 1972. For more information, see Damon.

8. I am indebted to Odessa Rose for calling this original title to my attention.

9. This ending mirrors Hansberry's own experiences; when she was eight years old, her parents moved the family into a wealthy, all-white neighborhood. They were met with threats, verbal harassment, and violent attacks. After an Illinois court evicted them in 1938, her father, Carl, enlisted the help of the NAACP to challenge restrictive real-estate covenants based on race; they took the case to the Supreme Court and won. Carl spent much of his time—and his own money—in Washington, while her mother, Nannie, defended the family against mob violence with a loaded shotgun. Although her father's court case was well known, had audiences known of her mother's actions, they might have been less likely to assume that Mama was expecting a happy ending in the family's move.

10. Hansberry never finished the play to her liking (Nemiroff completed the play for her after her death, compiling finished drafts and earlier fragments of scenes and, when necessary, adding material based on his discussions with her). The play was not staged during her lifetime, although the Actors Studio Writers' Workshop staged a scene in 1963 that Nemiroff claims "was one of the most extraordinary sessions ever held at the Studio" and "confirmed [Hansberry's] sense of the power of what was already on paper" (*Lorraine* 33).

CHAPTER 5

1. However, the novel does try to humanize prostitution. In the case of Laura Saunders, for example, the authors show the economic circumstance that led her to become a prostitute, and she engages in political discussions with Billy, arguing for the democratic necessity for the MWIU.

2. Vigano's short-story collection, *Matrimonio in brigata*, was published for the first time in English as *Partisan Wedding* in 1999, by the University of Missouri Press. The collection explores the theme of how war is fought on the personal level.

EPILOGUE

1. In their excellent oral history collection, *Tender Comrades: A Backstory of the Hollywood Blacklist* (1997), Patrick McGilligan and Paul Buhle record the effects of McCarthyism on the blacklistees. They claim that the HUAC campaign against the Hollywood Left severely limited the production of films that were not Soviet propaganda but "stories suffused with feeling for people and their ordinary concerns" (xix). According to Alvah Bessie, a scriptwriter and member of the Hollywood Ten, HUAC fragmented what had otherwise been a strong and cohesive Communist Party organization: "There must have been two or three hundred people in the talent and crafts section alone, not counting the backlots and so forth. But they didn't stand up too well once the blacklist hit. People began avoiding you, people began crossing the street when they saw you—people with whom you had associated for years" (qtd. in McGilligan and Buhle 107).

2. Between 1924 and 1946, Le Sueur published eighty-six short stories, articles, poems, and reviews (the vast majority in non–Communist Party publications). See Pratt 255.

3. For a fuller account of this community, see Patrick McGilligan and Paul Buhle, *Tender Comrades: A Backstory of the Hollywood Blacklist;* and Rebecca M. Schreiber, *Cold War Exiles in Mexico: US Dissidents and the Culture of Critical Resistance.*

4. Friedan's obituary in *New York Times* claims that at the time she wrote *The Feminine Mystique,* "she was a suburban housewife and mother who supplemented her husband's income by writing freelance articles for women's magazines" (Fox). While her time with the *UE News* is mentioned, nothing is said about her Left feminist publications with the paper. The *Times* obituary is typical; the one notable exception I have been able to find is the *Washington Post* obituary, which does quote Horowitz in an effort to ground Friedan's work in the Left/labor movements of the 1940s (Sullivan).

5. Historian Gerda Lerner praised *The Feminine Mystique* at the time of its publication, but she also criticized Friedan's failure to include black and working-class women (in Rosen 5–6).

6. When I introduced myself to Olsen at a reading a few years before her death and explained my project, she immediately expressed her desire to be involved and took the time to answer my questions and offer insights, even though it was late and she had been signing books and responding to questions for several hours. Olsen made researching the Old Left much easier for a number of people because of her willingness to talk and write openly about her own experiences.

Works Cited

Aaron, Daniel. *Writers on the Left: Episodes in American Literary Communism*. 1961. New York: Columbia UP, 1992.

Abramson, Doris E. *Negro Playwrights in the American Theatre, 1925–1959*. New York: Columbia UP, 1969.

Aldridge, Jack. "As to Academic Freedom." Rev. of *The Searching Light*, by Martha Dodd. *St. Louis Post-Dispatch* 31 Mar. 1955. Press Clippings File 12.6. Dodd Papers.

Anthony II, Susan B. "Out of the Kitchen—Into the War." Litof 213–18.

Aptheker, Herbert. "The Negro Woman." *Masses and Mainstream* 2.1 (1949): 10–17.

Armstrong, Nancy. "Introduction: Literature as Women's History." *Genre* 19 (1986): 347–69.

Arnow, Harriette. *The Dollmaker*. New York: Hearst, 1954.

Austin, Gayle. "Alice Childress: Black Woman Playwright as Feminist Critic." *Southern Quarterly* 25.3 (1997): 53–62.B., Harold. "Fight for Women's Rights Impractical." Letter. *Daily Worker* 13 June 1948: 9.

Babb, Sanora. "Femme Fatale." *Masses and Mainstream* 1.1 (1948): 56–62.

———. *The Lost Traveler*. Albuquerque: U of New Mexico P, 1995.

Balthaser, Benjamin. "Cold War Revisions: Representation and Resistance in the Unseen Salt of the Earth." *American Quarterly* 60.2 (2008): 347–71.

Barson, Michael, and Steven Heller. *Red Scared: The Commie Menace in Propaganda and Popular Culture*. San Francisco: Chronicle, 2001.

Barzman, Norma. *The Red and the Blacklist: The Intimate Memoir of a Hollywood Expatriate*. New York: Nation Books, 2003.

Baxandall, Rosalyn. "The Question Seldom Asked: Women and the CPUSA." *New Studies in the Politics and Culture of US Communism*. Ed. Michael Brown et al. New York: Monthly Review P, 1993. 141–61.

———. *Words on Fire: The Life and Writing of Elizabeth Gurley Flynn*. New Brunswick: Rutgers UP, 1987.

Boyd, Herb. "Peekskill Riots." Buhle, Buhle, and Georgakas, *Encyclopedia* 572–73.

Boyer, Richard O. Rev. of *Home Is the Sailor*, by Beth McHenry and Frederick M. Myers. *Masses and Mainstream* 1.8 (1948): 73.

Brill, Margaret. "Can You Help This Wife?" Letter. *Daily Worker* 6 June 1948: 2:9.

Brody, Lillian. "Male Supremacy, an Anti-Labor Device." *Worker* 4 Mar. 1951: 4–5.

Brown, Lloyd L. *Iron City*. 1951. Boston: Northeastern, 1994.

Brown-Guillory, Elizabeth. "Black Women Playwrights: Exorcising Myths." *Phylon* 48.3 (1987): 229–39.

———. "Images of Blacks in Plays by Black Women." *Phylon* 47.3 (1986): 230–37.

———. *Their Place on the Stage: Black Women Playwrights in America*. New York: Greenwood, 1988.

Brysac, Shareen Blair. *Resisting Hitler: Mildred Harnack and the Red Orchestra*. New York: Oxford UP, 2000.

Buhle, Mary Jo. *Women and the American Left: A Guide to Sources*. Boston: G. K. Hall, 1983.

Buhle, Mari Jo, Paul Buhle, and Dan Georgakas, eds. *Encyclopedia of the American Left*. Urbana: U of Illinois P, 1992.

Buhle, Paul. *Marxism in the United States: Remapping the History of the American Left*. London: Verso, 1991.

"Call Negro Women to 'Sojourn for Justice.'" *Daily Worker* 20 Sept. 1951: 5.

Carter, Steven R. *Hansberry's Drama: Commitment amid Complexity*. Urbana: U of Illinois P, 1991.

Childress, Alice. "But I Do My Own Thing: Can Black and White Artists Still Work Together?" *New York Times* 2 Feb. 1969: D1+.

————. "A Candle in a Gale Wind." Evans 111–16.

————. "A Conversation from Life." *Freedom* Jan. 1954: 4.

————. *Florence. Masses and Mainstream* 3.10 (1950): 34–47.

————. "For a Negro Theater" *Masses and Mainstream* 4.2 (1951): 61–64.

————. *Like One of the Family: Conversations from a Domestic's Life*. 1956. Boston: Beacon, 1986.

————. "The 'Many Others' In History: A Conversation from Life." *Freedom* Feb. 1952: 2.

————. "The Negro Woman in American Literature." *Freedomways* 6.1 (1966): 14–19.

————. "Old Master Said to Jim: 'You Got Your Faults and I Got Mine.'" *Freedom* Aug. 1954: 8.

————. *Trouble in Mind* (original version). *Black Theatre: A Twentieth Century Collection of the Work of Its Best Playwrights*. Ed. Lindsay Patterson. New York: Plume, 1971. 207–69.

————. *Trouble in Mind* (revised three-act version). 1970 ms. DU78027. Copyright division, Library of Congress, Washington, DC.

————. "What Does Africa Want? Freedom!" *Freedom* June 1953: 12.

Citron, Alice. "Searching Light on a University." Rev. of *The Searching Light*, by Martha Dodd. *National Guardian* 2 May 1955. Press Clippings File 12.6. Dodd Papers.

Coiner, Constance. *Better Red: The Writing and Resistance of Tillie Olsen and Meridel Le Sueur*. 1995. Urbana: U of Illinois P, 1998.

Congress of American Women. *Ten Women Anywhere Can Start Anything*. New York [pamphlet, Sophia Smith collection].

————. "What Is the Congress of American Women?" New York [pamphlet, Sophia Smith collection].

Coontz, Stephanie. *The Way We Never Were: American Families and the Nostalgia Trap*. New York: Basic, 1992.

Cott, Nancy. *The Grounding of Modern Feminism*. New Haven: Yale UP, 1989.

Dale, Thema. "Reconversion and the Negro People." *Political Affairs* Oct. 1945: 899.

Damon, Gene. "The Ladder, Rung by Rung." Introduction. *The Ladder* 1–2. New York: Arno, 1975. i–iii.

Davidman, Joy. "Women: Hollywood Version." *New Masses* 17 Jun. 1942: 28.

Davies, Carol Boyce. *Left of Karl Marx: The Political Life of Black Communist Claudia Jones*. Durham, NC: Duke UP, 2008.

Davis, Angela Y. *Women, Race, and Class*. New York: Random House, 1983.

Davis, Arthur P. "Integration and Race Literature." *The American Negro Writer and His Roots*. New York: AMSAC, 1960: 34–40.

Davis, Ossie. "The Significance of Lorraine Hansberry." *Freedomways* 5.3 (1965): 397–402.

Dengel, Veronica. Profile. *New Yorker*. Rpt. in *Masses and Mainstream* 1.8 (1948): 71.

Denning, Michael. *The Cultural Front*. London: Verso, 1997.

Dennis, Peggy. *Autobiography of an American Communist: A Personal View of a Political Life.* Berkeley: Lawrence Hill, 1977.

———. "Comradely Yours." *Sunday Worker* 1 Apr. 1951: 4.

Dodd, Martha. Biographical Note for *The Searching Light.* Ms. 12.7. Dodd Papers.

———. "Biography of William Dodd, Sr." Ms. 2.13. Dodd Papers.

———. "Daughter of Earth." Ms. 10.24. Dodd Papers.

———. "Hoyerswerda: Socialist New Town." *World News* 27 Feb. 1960: 107–12.

———. "Imprison a Flame?" Ms. 11.3. Dodd Papers.

———. Letter to Charles Humboldt. 30 April 1959. Correspondence File 12.18. Dodd Papers.

———. Letter to David Klopfer. 27 Apr. 1981. Correspondence File 6.2. Dodd Papers.

———. Letter to D. N. Pritt. 20 June 1959. Correspondence File 8.10. Dodd Papers.

———. "Maria." *Masses and Mainstream* 3.10 (1950): 19–25.

———. Martha Eccles Dodd Papers. Library of Congress, Washington, DC.

———. "Paul Robeson." *Mainstream* 16.5 (1963): 53–56.

———. "Poet's Wife." Ms. 14.18. Dodd Papers.

———. Press clippings file. 2.15. Dodd Papers.

———. "Prisoner #4678860." Ms. 11.3. Dodd Papers.

———. "Reflections on a Novel." Ms. 12.11. Dodd Papers.

———. *The Searching Light.* New York: Citadel, 1955.

———. *Sowing the Wind.* New York: Harcourt, 1945.

———. *Through Embassy Eyes.* New York: Harcourt, 1939.

———. "To Those Who Sit in Darkness." Ms. 11.31. Dodd Papers.

———. "The Twain Have Met." Ms. 11.32. Dodd Papers.

———. "Waiting at Poprad, CSSR." Ms. 11.37. Dodd Papers.

———. "World Without Weapons." Ms. 11.41. Dodd Papers.

Dodd, Martha, and Alfred K. Stern. Press Release. Prague, Czechoslovakia. 6 Sept. 1957. Ms. 13.4. Dodd Papers.

Duberman, Martin Bauml. *Paul Robeson.* New York: Knopf, 1988.

Dudziak, Mary L. *Cold War, Civil Rights: Race and the Image of American Democracy.* Princeton: Princeton UP, 2000.

Dziewanowski, M. K. *A History of Soviet Russia.* Englewood Cliffs, NJ: Prentice-Hall, 1985.

Egerton, John. *Speak Now against the Day: The Generation before the Civil Rights Movement in the South.* Chapel Hill: U of North Carolina P, 1994.

Einstein, Albert. Letter to Martha Dodd. 6 July 1953. Correspondence File 12.5. Dodd Papers.Epstein, Irene. "Women in the USSR." *Masses and Mainstream* 4.5 (1951): 92–94.

Evans, Mari, ed. *Black Women Writers (1950–1980): A Critical Evaluation.* Garden City, NJ: Anchor, 1984.

Evans, Sara. *Personal Politics: The Roots of Women's Liberation in the Civil Rights Movement and the New Left.* New York: Random, 1980.

Farnham, Marynia F., and Ferdinand Lundberg. *Modern Woman: The Lost Sex.* New York: Harper, 1947.

Farrell, James J. *The Spirit of the Sixties: The Making of Postwar Radicalism.* New York: Routledge, 1997.

Federal Bureau of Investigation (FBI). Alice Childress File. Freedom of Information/Privacy Acts 0933046-000.

———. Lorraine Hansberry File. Freedom of Information/Privacy Acts 0933051-000.

Feuchtwanger, Lion. "Mirror of America." Rev. of *The Searching Light*, by Martha Dodd. *Nation* 9 July 1955. Press Clippings File 12.6. Dodd Papers.

Flexner, Eleanor. *Century of Struggle*. 1959. Cambridge, MA: Harvard UP, 1996.

Flynn, Elizabeth Gurley. "Hitler's 3 K's for Woman—An American Rehash." *Political Affairs* 26.4 (1947). Rpt. in Baxandall, *Words* 202–8.

———. "Life of the Party." *Daily Worker* 7 June 1948: 10.

———. "What *Salt of the Earth* Means to Me." *Political Affairs* June 1954: 63–65.

———. *Woman's Place—in the Fight for a Better World*. New York: New Century, 1947.

———. *Women in the War*. New York: Workers Library, 1942. Rpt. in Baxandall, *Words* 187–96.

Foley, Barbara. *Radical Representations: Politics and Form in US Proletarian Fiction, 1929–1941*. Durham: Duke UP, 1993.

Foster, William Z. "On Improving the Party's Work among Women." *Political Affairs* 27.11 (1948): 984–90.

Fox, Margalit. "Betty Friedan, Who Ignited Cause in 'Feminine Mystique,' Dies at 85." *New York Times* 5 Feb. 2006: n.p. Web. 6 Feb. 2006.

Friedan, Betty. *The Feminine Mystique*. 1963. New York: Bantam, 1983.

Gaines, Kevin. "From Center to Margin: Internationalism and the Origins of Black Feminism." *Materializing Democracy: Toward a Revitalized Cultural Politics*. Ed. Russ Castronovo and Dana D. Nelson. Durham: Duke UP, 2002. 294–313.

Georgakas, Dan. "Taft-Hartley Loyalty Oath." Buhle, Buhle, and Georgakas, *Encyclopedia* 767–70.

Gerson, Joan. "Can a Housewife Be Politically Active?" *Daily Worker* 21 April 1948: 11.

Gilkes, Lillian B., Papers. Special Collections Research Center, Syracuse University Library, Syracuse, NY.

Gore, Dayo F. *Radicalism at the Crossroads: African American Women Activists in the Cold War*. New York: New York U P, 2011.

Gornick, Vivian. *The Romance of American Communism*. New York: Basic, 1977.

Graham, Shirley. *The Story of Phillis Wheatley*. New York: Julian Messner, 1949.

Gregory, Yvonne. "Beulah Richardson: Poet Demands Equality for Negro Womanhood." *Freedom* 1.9 (1951): 7.

———. "Cincinnati Notebook." *Masses and Mainstream* 4.12 (1951): 40–42.

———. "Mrs. Ingram's Kinfolks." *Masses and Mainstream* 4.11 (1951): 8–14.

Haber, Leila. "A Look at the Big 3 in Women's Magazines." *Sunday Worker* 27 Dec. 1953: 8.

Hapke, Laura. *Labor's Text: The Worker in American Fiction*. New Brunswick, NJ: Rutgers UP, 2001.

Hansberry, Lorraine. "A Challenge to Artists." *Freedomways* 3.1 (1963): 33–35.

———. "CNA Presents Exciting New Review." *Freedom* May 1952: 7.

———. *The Drinking Gourd*. Nemiroff, *Lorraine* 163–217.

———. "Egyptian People Fight for Freedom." *Freedom* 2.3 (1952): 3.

———. "'Illegal' Conference Shows Peace Is Key to Freedom." *Freedom* 2.4 (1952): 3.

———. "In Defense of the Equality of Men." *The Norton Anthology of Literature by Women*. Ed. Sandra M. Gilbert and Susan Gubar. New York: Norton, 1985. 2058–67.

———. "Legacy of W.E.B. Du Bois." *Freedomways* 5.1 (1965): 20.

———. *Les Blancs*. Nemiroff, *Lorraine* 37–128.

———. "Negroes Cast in Same Old Roles in TV Shows." *Freedom* June 1951: 7.

———. "On Arthur Miller, Marilyn Monroe, and 'Guilt.'" Malpede 173–76.

———. "On Strinberg and Sexism." Malpede 171–73.

———. *A Raisin in the Sun*. 1958. New York: Random House, 1994.

———. "Report Back Rally." *Worker* 22 June 1952: 2:8.

———. "This Complex of Womanhood." *Ebony* 15.10 (1960): 40.

———. *To Be Young, Gifted and Black*. New York: New American, 1970.

———. "Village Intellect Revealed." *New York Times* 11 Oct. 1964, sec. 2:1+.

———. "Women Voice Demands in Capital Sojourn." *Freedom* Oct. 1951: 6.

Harris, Elise. "The Double Life of Lorraine Hansberry." *Out* Sept. 1999: 96+.

Harris, Trudier. *From Mammies to Militants: Domestics in Black American Literature*. Philadelphia: Temple UP, 1982.

———. Introduction. Childress, *Like One of the Family* xi–xxxiv.

Healey, Dorothy, and Maurice Isserman. *Dorothy Healey Remembers: A Life in the American Communist Party*. New York: Oxford, 1990.

Hedges, Elaine. Introduction. *Ripening: Selected Work*. By Meridel Le Sueur. New York: Feminist P, 1982. 1–28.

Hellman, Lillian. *Scoundrel Time*. Boston: Little, Brown, 1976.

Henderson, Mae Gwendolyn. "Speaking in Tongues: Dialogics, Dialectics, and the Black Woman Writer's Literary Tradition." *Reading Black, Reading Feminist: A Critical Anthology*. Ed. Henry Louis Gates Jr. New York: Penguin, 1990. 116–42.

Hennessy, Rosemary, and Chrys Ingraham, eds. *Materialist Feminism: A Reader in Class, Difference, and Women's Lives*. New York: Routledge, 1997.

Hill, Rebecca. "Fosterites and Feminists, or 1950s Ultra-Leftists and the Invention of AmeriKKKa," *New Left Review* 228 (1998): 67–90.

Honey, Maureen. *Creating Rosie the Riveter: Class, Gender, and Propaganda during World War II*. Amherst: U of Massachusetts P, 1985.

Horne, Gerald. *Black Liberation/Red Scare: Ben Davis and the Communist Party*. Newark: U of Delaware P, 1994.

———. "Civil Rights Congress." Buhle, Buhle, and Georgakas, *Encyclopedia* 134–35.

Horowitz, Daniel. *Betty Friedan and the Making of* The Feminine Mystique: *The American Left, The Cold War, and Modern Feminism*. Amherst: U of Massachusetts P, 1998.

———. "Rethinking Betty Friedan." *American Quarterly* (March 1996): 1–31.

"Household Helpers Find It's Time to Help Themselves." *Worker* 12 June 1949: 5.

Hughes, Langston. *Selected Poems of Langston Hughes*. New York: Random, 1987.

Isserman, Maurice. *If I Had a Hammer: The Death of the Old Left and the Birth of the New Left*. Urbana: U of Illinois P, 1993.

————. *Which Side Were You On? The American Communist Party during the Second World War*. Urbana: U of Illinois P, 1993.

Jarrico, Paul. "Chronology of Events." M. Wilson 185–87.

Jarrico, Paul, and Herbert J. Biberman. "Breaking Ground." M. Wilson 169–74.

Jarrico, Sylvia. "Evil Heroines of 1953." *Hollywood Review* 1 (1953): 1, 3–4.

Jennings, La Vinia Delois. *Alice Childress*. New York: Simon and Schuster, 1995.

Jones, Claudia. "Discussion Article." *Political Affairs* 24.8 (1945): 717–20.

————. "An End to the Neglect of the Problems of the Negro Woman!" *Political Affairs* 28.6 (1949): 51–67.

————. "For New Approaches to Our Work among Women." *Political Affairs* 27.8 (1948): 738–43.

————. "Foster's Political and Theoretical Guidance to Our Work among Women." *Political Affairs* 30.3 (1951): 68–78.

————. "Sojourners for Truth and Justice." *Worker* 10 Feb. 1952: 8.

————. "We Seek Full Equality for Women." *Sunday Worker* 4 Sept. 1949: 11.

Jones, John Hudson. "An Evaluation of the American Negro Theatre." *Daily Worker* 25 Aug. 1946: 14.

Just a Little Simple. Playbill. 1950. Clipping File, Part II, 1975–1988, fiche 903. Schomburg Center for Research in Black Culture, New York.

Kelley, Robin D. G. *Freedom Dreams: The Black Radical Imagination*. Boston: Beacon, 2002.

————. *Hammer and Hoe: Alabama Communists during the Great Depression*. Chapel Hill: U of North Carolina P, 1990.

Klehr, Harvey. *The Heyday of American Communism: The Depression Decade*. New York: Basic, 1984.

Krumbein, Margaret. "How to Fight for Women's Rights." *Daily Worker* 8 Aug. 1948: 2:9

Kuznick, Peter J., and James Gilbert, eds. *Rethinking Cold War Culture*. Washington, DC: Smithsonian, 2001.

Larson, Erik. *In the Garden of Beasts: Love, Terror, and an American Family in Hitler's Berlin*. New York, Crown, 2011.

Lawson, John Howard. *Film in the Battle of Ideas*. New York: Masses and Mainstream, 1953.

Lazarus, Helen. "What's New in Women's Magazines." *Masses and Mainstream* 7.10 (1954): 40–45.

Lee, Spike. "Commentary: Thoughts on the Screenplay." Nemiroff, *Raisin* xlv–xlvii.

The Legacy of the Hollywood Blacklist. Dir. Judy Chakin. One Step Productions, 1987.

Lerner, Gerda. *Fireweed: A Political Autobiography*. Philadelphia: Temple UP, 2002.

Lester, Julius. "The Voice and Vision of Lorraine Hansberry: The Politics of Caring." Nemiroff, *Lorraine* 262–75.

Le Sueur, Meridel. *Crusaders*. New York: Blue Heron P, 1955.

————. *Harvest Song: Collected Essays and Stories*. Albuquerque: West End, 1990.

————. *Ripening: Selected Work*. New York: Feminist P, 1982.

————. "You Belong in the Family of the Free." *Worker* 28 Apr. 1946: 11.

L.H.N. Letter. *The Ladder* 1.8 (1957): 26–28.

Litof, Judy Barrett, and David C. Smith, eds. *American Women in a World at War: Contemporary Accounts from World War II*. Wilmington, DE: Scholarly Resources, 1977.

L. N. Letter. *The Ladder* 1.11 (1957): 30.

Lorde, Audre. *Zami: A New Spelling of My Name*. Freedom, CA: Crossing P, 1982.

Malpede, Karen, ed. *Women in Theatre: Compassion and Hope*. New York: Drama Book Publishers, 1983.Maltz, Albert. Letter to Martha Dodd. Correspondence File 7.7 Dodd Papers.

Marshall, Paule. *Brown Girl, Brownstones*. 1959. New York: Feminist, 1981.

Maxwell, William J. *New Negro, Old Left: African-American Writing and Communism between the Wars*. New York: Columbia UP, 1999.

May, Elaine Tyler. *Homeward Bound: American Families in the Cold War Era*. New York: Basic, 1999.

———. *Pushing the Limits: American Women, 1940–1961*. New York: Oxford UP, 1994.

May, Larry, ed. *Recasting America: Culture and Politics in the Age of the Cold War*. Chicago: U of Chicago P, 1989.

McDuffie, Erik S. "'No Small Amount of Change Could Do': Esther Cooper Jackson and the Making of a Black Left Feminist." *Want to Start a Revolution? Radical Women in the Black Freedom Struggle*. Ed. Dayo F. Gore, Jeanne Theoharis, and Komozi Woodard. New York: New York UP, 2009. 25–46.

———. *Sojourning for Freedom: Black Women, American Communism, and the Making of Black Left Feminism*. Durham, NC: Duke UP, 2011.

McGilligan, Patrick, and Paul Buhle. *Tender Comrades: A Backstory of the Hollywood Blacklist*. New York: St. Martin's, 1997.

McHenry, Beth, and Frederick M. Myers. *Home Is the Sailor*. New York: International Publishers, 1948.

Merriam, Eve. "Genevieve Taggard." *Masses and Mainstream* 2.1 (1949): 55.

———. "Spring Cleaning." *Masses and Mainstream* 5.3 (1952): 17–19.

Meyer, Gerald. "American Labor Party." Buhle, Buhle, and Georgakas, *Encyclopedia* 24–25.

———. "Gay/Lesbian Liberation Movement." Buhle, Buhle, and Georgakas, *Encyclopedia* 257–65.

Meyerowitz, Joanne. *Not June Cleaver: Women and Gender in Postwar America, 1956–1960*. Philadelphia: Temple UP, 1994.

Millard, Betty. *Woman against Myth*. New York: International, 1948.

Mitchell, Loften. "The Negro Writer and His Materials." *The American Negro Writer and His Roots*. New York: AMSAC, 1960: 55–60.

———. "Three Writers and a Dream." *Crisis* 72 (1965): 219–23.

Mitgang, Herbert. "Books of the Times." Rev. of *The Searching Light*, by Martha Dodd. *New York Times* 26 Mar. 1955. Press Clippings File 12.6. Dodd Papers.

M. L. "Housewife in Position of Unorganized Worker." Letter. *Daily Worker* 13 June 1948: 9.

Moos, Elizabeth. "Women for Peace." *Masses and Mainstream* 4.6 (1951): 46–56.

"Morros Testified Mrs. Stern Spied for Soviet Hire." *New York Times* 18 Aug. 1957: 1:1+.

Nadel, Alan. *Containment Culture: American Narratives, Postmodernism, and the Atomic Age*. Durham: Duke UP, 1995.

Naison, Mark. *Communists in Harlem during the Depression*. Urbana: U of Illinois P, 1983.

Nekola, Charlotte, and Paula Rabinowitz, eds. *Writing Red: An Anthology of American Women Writers, 1930–1940*. New York: Feminist, 1987.

Nemiroff, Robert, ed. *Lorraine Hansberry: The Collected Last Plays*. New York: Plume, 1983.

———, ed. *A Raisin in the Sun: The Original Unfilmed Screenplay*. New York: Penguin, 1992.

Newton, Judith, and Deborah Rosenfelt, eds. *Feminist Criticism and Social Change: Sex, Class, and Race in Literature and Culture*. New York: Methuen, 1985.

Olsen, Tillie. *Silences*. 1978. New York: Feminist P, 2003.

———. *Tell Me a Riddle*. New York: Dell, 1994.

Page, Myra. *Daughter of the Hills*. 1950. New York: Feminist P, 1977.

Paley, Grace. *The Little Disturbances of Man*. 1959. New York: Penguin, 1985.

Perkins, Kathy A. E-mail to author. 8 May 2009.

Petry, Ann. *Harriet Tubman: Conductor of the Underground Railroad*. 1955. New York: Harper Collins, 1996.

———. *The Street*. 1946. Boston: Houghton, 1974.

Pitts, Ethel. "The American Negro Theatre: 1940–1949." Diss. U of Missouri–Columbia, 1975.

Popova, Nina. "Women under Socialism." *Worker* 5 Nov. 1950: 4.

Pratt, Linda Ray. "Woman Writer in the CP: The Case of Meridel Le Sueur." *Women's Studies* 14.3 (1988): 247–64.

"Preface for Today." *Masses and Mainstream* 1.1 (1948): 1.

Rabinowitz, Paula. *Labor and Desire: Women's Revolutionary Fiction in Depression America*. Chapel Hill: U of North Carolina P, 1991.

Reiner, Margrit. "The Fictional American Woman: A Look at Some Recent Novels." *Masses and Mainstream* 5.6 (1952): 1–10.

———. "Morning." *Masses and Mainstream* 4.3 (1951): 45–52.

———. "The Petition." *Masses and Mainstream* 5.9 (1952): 44–51.

Rella, Ettore. "These Treasures in the Earth." *Masses and Mainstream* 5.8 (1952): 15–16.

Richardson, Beulah. *A Black Woman Speaks*. New York: American Women for Peace, 1951.

Rich, Adrienne. "The Problem with Lorraine Hansberry." *Freedomways* 19.4 (1979): 247–55.

Robertson, Nan. "Dramatist Against the Odds." *New York Times* 8 Mar. 1959: 2:3.

Roosevelt, Eleanor. "Two Books." Rev. of *The Searching Light*, by Martha Dodd. *New York World-Telegram* 23 Aug. 1945. Press Clippings File 12.6. Dodd Papers.

Rose, Odessa. "'Happenstance and Unpredictables' in Lorraine Hansberry's *A Raisin in the Sun*." Unpublished essay, 1998.

Rosen, Ruth. *The World Split Open: How the Modern Women's Movement Changed America*. New York: Penguin, 2000.

Rosenfelt, Deborah Silverton. Afterword. *Daughter of the Hills*. By Myra Page. New York: Feminist, 1986. 247–68.

———. Commentary. M. Wilson, *Salt* 93–168.

———. "From the Thirties: Tillie Olsen and the Radical Tradition." *Feminist Studies* 7 (1981): 371–406.

———. "Getting into the Game: American Women Writers and the Radical Tradition." *Women's Studies International Forum* 9.4 (1986): 363–72.

———. "Rereading *Tell Me a Riddle* in the Age of Deconstruction." *Listening to Silences: New Essays in Feminist Criticism*. Ed. Elaine Hedges and Shelley Fisher Fishkin. New York: Oxford UP, 1994. 49–70.

Rothschild, Matthew. "The New McCarthyism." *The Progressive* 66.1 (2002): 18–23.

Rubinstein, Annette. "Scholar as Hero." Rev. of *The Searching Light*, by Martha Dodd. *Masses and Mainstream* 8.6 (1955): 63

Rupp, Leila J., and Verta Taylor. *Survival in the Doldrums: The American Women's Rights Movement, 1945 to the 1960s.* New York: Oxford UP, 1987.

Scandalize My Name: Stories from the Blacklist. Dir. Alexandra M. Isles. 2000.

Schaub, Thomas Hill. *American Fiction in the Cold War.* Madison: U of Wisconsin P, 1991.

Schleuning, Neala. *America: Song We Sang Without Knowing.* Mankato, MN: Little Red Hen, 1983.

Schrecker, Ellen. *Many Are the Crimes: McCarthyism in America.* Boston: Little, Brown, 1998.

———. *No Ivory Tower: McCarthyism and the Universities.* New York: Oxford UP, 1986.

Schreiber, Rebecca M. *Cold War Exiles in Mexico: US Dissidents and the Culture of Critical Resistance.* Minneapolis: U of Minnesota P, 2008.

ScotTissue. Advertisement.

Segal, Edith. "Negro Child to It's Mother." *Masses and Mainstream* 2.6 (1949): 69.

Seghers, Anna. "The Delegate's Daughter." *Masses and Mainstream* 5.7 (1952): 39–49.

Sillen, Samuel. "Behind the Ivy Curtain." *Masses and Mainstream* 2.3 (1949): 7–17.

———. *Women against Slavery.* New York: Masses and Mainstream, 1955.

Sinclair, Jo. *The Changelings.* 1955. New York: Feminist P, 1985.

Smethurst, James Edward. *The New Red Negro: The Literary Left and African American Poetry, 1930–1946.* New York: Oxford UP, 1999.

———. "SNYC, *Freedomways*, and the Influence of the Popular Front in the South on the Black Arts Movement." *Reconstruction: Studies in Contemporary Culture* 8.1 (2008): n.p. Web. 3 Aug. 2009.

Smith, Lucy. "The Lesson." *Masses and Mainstream* 7.2 (1954): 12–13.

Smith, Valerie. *Not Just Race, Not Just Gender: Black Feminist Readings.* New York: Routledge, 1998.

"Sojourners for Truth Hold Brooklyn Meeting." *Daily Worker* 29 June 1952: 8.

Steinberg, Ruth. "One Enchanted Evening." *Masses and Mainstream* 6.9 (1953): 11–21.

Sterling, Dorothy. "Four Score and More." Unpublished ms.

———. *Freedom Train: The Story of Harriet Tubman.* 1954. New York: Scholastic, 1987.

———. Personal interview. 30 Sept. 2000.

Sullivan, Patricia. "Betty Friedan, 1921-2006: Voice of Feminism's 'Second Wave.'" *Washington Post* 5 Feb. 2006: n.p. Web. 6 Feb. 2006.

Swerdlow, Amy. "The Congress of American Women: Left-Feminist Peace Politics in the Cold War." *US History as Women's History: New Feminist Essays.* Ed. Linda K. Kerber, Alice Kessler-Harris, and Kathryn Kish Sklar. Chapel Hill: U of North Carolina P, 1995. 296–312, 429–34.

"Three Women of Leningrad." *Daily Worker* 8 Mar. 1950: 5.

Tuttle, William M., Jr. "America's Children in an Era of War, Hot and Cold: The Holocaust, the Bomb, and Child Rearing in the 1940s." Kuznick 14–34.

Vigano, Renata. "Agnes." *Masses and Mainstream* 7.3 (1954): 21–27.

Vogel, Lise, ed. "Red Feminism: A Symposium." *Science and Society* 66.4 (2002–2003): 498–535.

Wald, Alan. "The Costs of McCarthyism." *Against the Current* 15.1 (2000): 31–38.

———. *Exiles from a Future Time: The Forging of the Mid-Twentieth-Century Left.* Chapel Hill: U of North Carolina P, 2002.

———. Foreword. Brown, *Iron City* vii–xxxvii.

———. Introduction. *Cry of the Tinamou.* By Sanora Babb. Lincoln: U of Nebraska P, 1998.

————. "Marxist Literary Resistance to the Cold War," *Prospects: An Annual of American Cultural Studies* 20 (1996): 479–92.

————. *Writing From the Left: New Essays on Radical Culture and Politics.* London: Verso, 1994.

Washington, Mary Helen. "Alice Childress, Lorraine Hansberry, and Claudia Jones: Black Women Write the Popular Front." *Left of the Color Line: Race, Radicalism, and Twentieth-Century Literature of the United States.* Ed. Bill V. Mullen and James Smethurst. Chapel Hill: U of North Carolina P, 2003.

————. Lecture. University of Maryland, College Park. 1 May 1998.

————. Personal interviews. 15 Aug. 2001; 20 Nov. 2001; 24 Apr. 2002.

Weigand, Kate. *Red Feminism: American Communism and the Making of Women's Liberation.* Baltimore: Johns Hopkins UP, 2001.

Weinstein, Allen and Alexander Vassiliev. *The Haunted Wood: Soviet Espionage in America—the Stalin Era.* New York: Random House, 1999.

"What Maternity Care Means." *Daily Worker* 5 Mar. 1950: 2:11.

Wheeler, Elizabeth A. *Uncontained: Urban Fiction in Postwar America.* New Brunswick, NJ: Rutgers UP, 2001.

Whitfield, Stephen J. *The Culture of the Cold War.* Baltimore: Johns Hopkins UP, 1996.

Wilkerson, Margaret. "The Dark Vision of Lorraine Hansberry: Excerpts from a Literary Biography." *Massachusetts Review* 28.4 (1987): 642–50.

————. "Excavating Our History: The Importance of Biographies of Women of Color." *Black American Literature Forum* 24.1 (1990): 73–84.

Williams, Raymond. *Marxism and Literature.* New York: Oxford UP, 177.

Wilson, Janet. "Negro Women Planted and Tended the Tree of Freedom." *Freedom* Feb. 1951: 7.

Wilson, Michael. *Salt of the Earth* (film prod. 1953). New York: Feminist P, 1978.

Wixson, Douglas. Introduction. *The Lost Traveler.* By Sanora Babb. Albuquerque: U of New Mexico P, 1995.

"Woman's Day in the War." *Worker* 4 Mar. 1945: 8.

"Women Active in Congress of Writers." *New York Evening Post* 31 May 1939: 4.

Worth, Robert F. "A Nation Defines Itself By Its Evil Enemies," *New York Times* 24 Feb. 2002: 4.1+.

Wright, Richard. *Native Son.* New York: Harper, 1940.

Index

CPSIA information can be obtained at www.ICGtesting.com
Printed in the USA
BVOW072224130612

292612BV00002B/2/P